"At one time or another, all of us have faced, are facing, or will face our 'Timothy moments' when discouragement, defeat, and fear are overwhelming. *When My Heart Is Faint* is a great reminder of the daily, moment-by-moment need for the transformational and healing power of the gospel of Jesus Christ in the lives of even the most seasoned Christ-follower."

GREG RICHARDSON, Executive Vice President/ Senior Credit Officer, Wells Fargo Bank, Los Angeles, California

"David Hegg is not only a skilled expositor, but also an experienced pastor and theologian. He so clearly connects the truth of the biblical text to the everyday struggles of ordinary Christians. He writes in a way that makes you feel as if you are having a conversation with him over coffee. As you read, you'll be encouraged and blessed."

RYAN STANLEY, Community Life Pastor, Veritas Community Church, Columbus, Ohio

"David Hegg's offering wonderfully illuminates the sustaining power of the gospel to those succumbing to fear and in danger of being redefined. May God encourage the feeble hearts with the power of the gospel."

SHAUN ABRAHAMS, Pastor & Church Planting Missionary, Killorglin Baptist Church, Republic of Ireland

"I can see the value of this book to pastors, leaders, and church members alike. This book reminds me that the gospel is for not only salvation, but also a guide to live life the way God intended it to be lived in this world. Like Timothy, I need to be continually immersed in the word so that I do not grow weary as I encounter the trials and difficulties of being in the world."

JEFF SMITH, Assistant District Manager Waste Connections Inc., Vancouver, Washington

"When My Heart is Faint is a fresh reminder we need to stop and reset our thinking about the gospel and all that it means. While each page is filled with carefully written insights into the truth about the gospel, Hegg hits the bull's eye when he summarizes the gospel as being all about God, first and foremost. That is what makes it — and this book — truly good news."

JIM LITCHFIELD, Principal, Ministry Financing Group, Huntington Beach, California

"We all have those days: when small problems become crises, when depression turns the world black, and spiritual discouragement overwhelms faith. David Hegg's new book *When My Heart Is Faint* is the antidote, offering words of surpassing strength, comfort, and encouragement for those difficult and demanding situations and seasons of life. More than a devotional, some parts of this book may surprise you, others remind you, but all of it will encourage you. Do yourself a favor: Read this book, and then keep it handy."

MARY HUNT, Author, Speaker, Founder, *Debt-Proof Living*

"*When My Heart Is Faint* reminds us just how transformative God's truth is. Hegg takes a healthy look at the gospel of Jesus Christ to show us the only true place spiritual refreshment can be found. As a missionary for the past 25 years, I am encouraged and refreshed. This is a necessary read for every Christian, as well as, for each man I disciple."

DON GORDON, Former Major League Baseball Pitcher, Director of International Baseball, SCORE International Chattanooga, Tennessee

"This world is distracting and can consume us believers if we focus upon the things that come with the world. This call to focus once again (and again and again…) upon the gospel is very refreshing and like visiting a dear old friend after a long separation. Hegg's comment on page 63 sums up the book well: "Paul is shouting to Timothy that he must stop focusing on the situations before him and get back to being enthralled with the Savior who has saved him." This is great counsel to us all at all times."

JODY EVANS, Vice President, Facilities and Office Services, Logix Federal Credit Union

"How many of us are perplexed, discouraged, or even a bit hopeless when we look at today's culture? In *When My Heart Is Faint* David Hegg shows how life's deeper questions and ultimate answers can be found in the gospel. He encourages us to look to God's Word, be brave enough to embrace our brokenness, and walk as new creatures in Jesus Christ. *When My Heart Is Faint* is a powerful reminder we are not alone in our struggles and we are renewed, refreshed, and truly free … all because of God's free grace."

FRANK SONTAG, Christian Apologist and Host, The Frank Sontag Show- KKLA, Los Angeles, CA

"In *When My Heart Is Faint*, David W. Hegg opens up to us the wonderful, rejuvenating vista of the gospel in a way that is as encouraging as it is understandable. By carefully examining Paul's encouragement to Timothy, David reminds us that God's grace is amazing and essential, not just to open the door to God's family, but also to be our constant source of strength and refreshment. In a time when life is almost unbearably busy and complicated for so many of us, this little book welcomes us to enjoy the "garden of God's grace in the gospel."

MARTHA HARDING, Director of Women's Ministries, **Grace Baptist Church, Santa Clarita, CA**

"For me, to sit under David's teaching is to feel the crook of the Shepherd's staff gently placed around my neck, tenderly drawing me to higher ground and greener pastures. This book is a perfect example. Here Paul's familiar words to Timothy come alive when seen through the perspective of spiritual weariness and drought. David offers more than a momentary word of encouragement, but instead provides a deep, reviving draw from the water of Life—God's Word. This book clarifies and refines gospel belief in a way that empowers gospel behavior."

MARTI WIEGMAN, Director of Women's Ministries, **Northpoint Church, Corona, CA**

"David Hegg does what many men (and pastors) are afraid to do, which is admit they're weak, vulnerable and in need of more than an occasional dosage of encouragement to help with life's escalating burdens. *When My Heart Is Faint* speaks into our spiritual fatigue by grounding us deeper in gospel truths as the answer for ongoing renewal and restoration."

RONNIE MARTIN, Founder and Lead Pastor, **Substance Church (EFCA), Ashland, Ohio, Author of *Stop Your Complaining***

WHEN MY HEART
IS FAINT

WHEN MY HEART IS FAINT

GOSPEL HELP WHEN LIFE GOES AWRY

DAVID W. HEGG

ABELAN PRESS

First published in the United States of America

Cover design: David Foglesong • davidfoglesong.com

All Bible references are from the English Standard Version (ESV), unless otherwise noted.

This book is dedicated to the wonderful staff of
Grace Baptist Church, Santa Clarita, California,
who first heard this material in our Chapel times
together. May the Lord continue to favor us
with His truth and love as we seek to make and
multiply Christ-followers who magnify the glory
of God. Our partnership in this great adventure
is a consistent source of joy and strength to me.

ACKNOWLEDGMENTS

Thanks go out to Pastor Stephen Davey and the staff of Colonial Baptist Church, Cary, North Carolina whose invitation to address them at their leadership conference gave me the chance to put these thoughts into a communicable form. I also appreciate the editorial effort of my assistant Martha Harding whose attention to detail and knowledge of theology always proves invaluable. Corona Mayhugh, my administrative assistant, has provided great support and encouragement, and managed my life so well that I had time to finish this project. Michele Puglisi added invaluable editorial assistance as well. Lastly, to my dear wife Cherylyn — my most trusted advisor and friend — I offer continued thanksgiving for partnering so well with me in life and in our ministry together for Christ's church.

CONTENTS

USING THIS BOOK

FOR PASTORS AND THOSE ENGAGED IN KINGDOM MINISTRY

As a pastor, I greatly resonate with Paul's words to Timothy during his years as a young pastor. Over my years of pastoral ministry, I have watched fellow pastors succumb to times of ministerial despair. Some have struggled through while others have walked away completely distraught, never to return. My hope is this little book can help in some way to ward off the ravages of circumstance that daily threaten to undermine pastoral ministry.

The church needs good men, and good men need every source of encouragement and help available. My prayer is Paul's short message to Timothy will be multiplied in its usefulness as the Spirit applies it to the hearts of those who, while attempting to lead the church, must remain vibrant, winsome, and valiant for truth.

FOR CHRIST-FOLLOWERS EVERYWHERE

As we all know, discouragement is an equal opportunity enemy. Every Christ-follower will face the temptation of spiritual discouragement somewhere along the path to glory. This book is written with them in mind additionally. My thinking is this: If Paul thought a gospel reminder would help Pastor Timothy regain his spiritual vitality in pagan Ephesus, then it must be powerful medicine for the rest of the church as well.

FOR THOSE DESIRING A SHORT THEOLOGICAL COURSE IN THE STORY OF JESUS CALLED THE GOSPEL

There is one more use of this book that may actually find the greatest audience. While addressing the challenges of discouragement in the lives of pastors and lay believers, you will also find a passionate, point-by-point re-telling of the gospel of Jesus. Maybe you know the gospel well. Maybe you think you know it well. Finally, maybe you know your knowledge of God's great story is sketchy and in need of being fleshed out biblically. Whatever the case, you are about to take a slow, guided tour through the beautiful landscape of God's gospel truth. Some parts may surprise you, others may remind you, while still others may encourage further study on your part. In the end, you will have a good overall grasp of the salvation God grants through the gospel, and as well, of the great encouragements found in daily resting in the garden of grace he alone provides.

So, whatever your place in the Kingdom of God, my hope is this book, and the gospel it describes, will meet you where you are and lead you where you need to be, by his grace, and for his glory!

INTRODUCTION

● ▬ ● ● ●

YOU NEED TO READ THIS

In Psalm 61:1–3, King David uses words and thoughts that often flood my own heart:

> ¹Hear my cry, O God, listen to my prayer; from the end of the earth I call to you when my heart is faint. ²Lead me to the rock that is higher than I, ³for you have been my refuge, a strong tower against the enemy.

Hear my cry, O God, listen to my prayer; from the end of the earth I call to you when my heart is faint. Even if this seems like an old-fashioned way of saying it, chances are you get the point. David knew what it was to be discouraged, even disconsolate due to challenges and circumstances beyond his control. I have struggled with these emotions, and I am sure you have as well.

Following Jesus Christ up the steep path of righteousness while the burdens of this broken world press down harder and harder is not for the faint hearted. The journey of faith takes its toil on even the most ardent disciple. Surely, you know what David felt like, seemingly at the end of the earth, calling out to the Lord, and thinking his voice just was not strong enough.

Can you remember a time when you felt that way? When life just kept piling on? You probably turned to God and prayed in ways that were deeper and more passionate than ever before. Yet, all you heard was silence. Maybe God slowly walked you out, but maybe you are still mired in the mud, uncertain as to what God has planned.

Now you are trying to regain confidence that God can be trusted in the tight spots. However, you have been in them for some time now, and it seems the rocks of discouragement just keep falling. Your head knows the right thing to feel, and do, but physically, emotionally, and spiritually you are just plain tired, worn thin, and almost worn out.

I have been there. Worse, I know I will be there again at some point, when adversity or my own stubbornness puts me in a place where God's chisel will be about the work of painstakingly forming Christ in me.

This book is my answer to those times when the waves are high, constant, and overwhelming, when spiritual fatigue truly sets in, and despair is hovering around the corner. The material here is not really mine. The biblical foundation started in the mind of God, was perfectly passed along by the Holy Spirit to the Apostle Paul, who intended it for a timid, burned-out pastor suffering from ministry shell-shock in the midst of a hostile culture. Moreover, being the word of the eternal God, it continues to be eternally relevant today, and that is great news.

What Paul wrote to Timothy is what I need today, and tomorrow, and for the rest of my life. If you are following Jesus closely, I know at some point you will need it too. In fact, today just might be the day you need some gospel help the most.

So, here it is in a nutshell: The gospel of Jesus Christ is more than the means of getting on the bus to heaven. It is the consistent, rejuvenating power by which the daily struggles and opportunities of this broken world may be recognized and turned to benefit. It truly is the help we all need when life goes awry.

Yes, the good news — the gospel — is the best medicine for the fainting heart. It is the most powerful antibiotic for the various spiritual infections that plague us in this life. And it has proven itself to be so for centuries, in the lives of millions who have turned to it time after time to reassert the fact that their identity is shaped and secured by the work of Christ, and not by the circumstances that surround them.

As the son of a pastor, I heard my dad explain the Lord's Supper hundreds of times. He often referred to Paul's declaration in 1 Corinthians 11:26: *For as often as you eat this bread and drink the cup, you proclaim the Lord's death until he comes.* It took me many years to understand what Paul meant. Even today, I am still growing in that understanding.

I am not talking about the controversies surrounding the bread and the cup that, ironically, have turned this demonstration of union with Christ into a divisive thing down through church history. What I really want to explore is this: to whom are we proclaiming the death of Christ, in the Supper?

Of course, as the church continues to see in the Supper the centrality of Christ crucified and risen, we proclaim to the world that the church is his and under his command. I believe there is another audience that is just as important. I believe in the Supper we proclaim the death of Christ to ourselves, and in so doing, bathe ourselves in the gospel every time. Or, at least we should!

Growing up, the gospel for me was really just the minimum amount of truth you had to believe in order to get on the bus to heaven. Once you grasped the gospel and believed it, you largely moved on from it to "weightier" topics like not going to movies, drinking wine, or dancing. It looked to me like the gospel was only for unbelievers, and after you believed, you forgot the gospel in order to focus on the laws of Christianity.

This line of thinking is backwards. God's law comes to unbelievers as a spotlight, illuminating their sin, uncovering their brokenness, and exposing their inability to live up to God's standard. That same light shines on Christ who stands in the middle of a glorious garden of grace we know as the gospel. As the Spirit enables us, we run to this garden and find rest. The law drove us here, but the gospel is where we dwell.

So, exactly what is this gospel? It is much more than a minimized, homogenized, dehydrated, 4-sentence sales pitch for team Jesus. It is the glorious story of God's redemptive plan, first hinted at in Genesis 3:15 and magnificently worked out to completion in the person and work of Jesus Christ.

Certainly in the Lord's Supper, we are proclaiming the gospel, and should be feeling its rejuvenating effects.

What about during other times? Like me, I am sure you know dry days when your soul seems parched, unfeeling, nearly deplete. Do you resonate with that? If so, what do you do when your heart feels faint?

I imagine, like me, you try to ignore it, or say a quick prayer asking for a spiritual alarm clock to go off and wake you from the doldrums. However, what if you go for several days with intermittent feelings that your spiritual fervor has been severely dampened?

I know folks who, when spiritually drained and in need of help first turn to their favorite praise and worship music. At times, I am one of them. Yet, as helpful as a favorite lyric or melody may be for the soul, it will be short lived. Long lasting rejuvenation demands something more substantial, something that not only pleases but also assails the heart and mind with the weight of God.

There are also times when my spiritual courage seems to fail me. Have you ever felt regret over your timidity in situations where boldness for Christ was called for? And how about when we are afraid? Afraid to stand for biblical principles at work or school? Reticent to enter into a conversation that really matters with a neighbor or seatmate on the airplane? And what about when obedience to Christ will mean being subjected to ridicule or worse?

However, spiritual fatigue and timidity are not the only conditions that prey on the Christ-follower's soul. The pervasive sadness that accompanies life in this world can often be overwhelming. Perhaps you are a single mother or father faced with raising your children to love Jesus while juggling the requirements of home, job, and social obligations. Or maybe employment has been elusive and financial pressures have created great stress on you and your family. Whatever the case — and if space allowed we could continue listing the ways life becomes almost unbearably sad — sometimes we all need to find a way out, to once again experience the light-hearted delight that comes from resting in the arms of Jesus.

All of these and more are situations and feelings we are faced with as we try to follow Jesus Christ closely. We want so much to be identified with him, yet at the same time we realize doing so is not easy. Battling our own deficiencies, our own sin, and our selfishness is hard enough without also having to deal with the circumstances this broken world throws in our way.

Paul said it well, in 2 Timothy 3:12: *Indeed, all who desire to live a godly life in Christ Jesus will be persecuted.* He was not speaking only of governmental opposition, but more about the ongoing warfare of living out the redeemed life, through as of yet, unredeemed flesh, in the midst of an unredeemed creation. To follow Christ closely is to run a grueling race, a marathon that demands we keep running even when fatigue, circumstance, and sadness hit like a hammer.

It is at these times we need a place to go, a refuge, a garden that offers spiritual rest and reformation. What we need, though we may not realize it, is the gospel freshly poured on us like cold water on parched lips.

This gospel is a rejuvenating truth that must become part of our daily spiritual intake as Christ-followers. Simply stated, we must preach the gospel to ourselves and do it regularly. We must settle down in this gracious garden and find rest for our souls from the daily circumstances of life. We must find in the gospel a retreat that refreshes our hearts, invigorates our minds, and circumscribes our plans and activities. Every day we need gospel help, for those daily times when life goes awry. As Fanny Crosby wrote:

> Jesus, keep me near the cross,
> There a precious fountain—
> Free to all, a healing stream—
> Flows from Calv'ry's mountain.
>
> In the cross, in the cross,
> Be my glory ever;
> Till my raptured soul shall find
> Rest beyond the river.

Crosby recognized what is too often lost on us today. She realized believers must live — every moment — near the cross. The cross — her shorthand for the whole redemptive plan of God — was her place for refreshing, the focus of her glorying, and the refuge where her soul found healing and help.

King David sought such a place as well. As God's King, he was subjected to criticism and opposition from every direction. Worse, his own heart warred against him time and time again. Through his writings, we see a common theme, a passionate desire to find rest and refuge. Psalm 61:1–3 was his declaration, that the only refuge worthy of life-long pursuit was the very presence of Almighty God:

> [1]Hear my cry, O God, listen to my prayer; [2]from the end of the earth I call to you when my heart is faint. Lead me to the rock that is higher than I, [3]for you have been my refuge, a strong tower against the enemy. (Psalm 61:1–3)

Today our refuge is that same place, that same Rock, our gracious and almighty God, into whose family we have been adopted. And, when life's waves begin to roll, threatening to dash us against the cliffs, it is to the gospel we must turn, to find firm footing for our souls on the rock that is higher than anything this world can throw at us.

While there are other sources of rejuvenation and reformation, which address the sins that can tear and weary the soul, no long-term health can happen without the gospel being primary in the mind and heart of the Christ-follower. For those maladies that trouble the soul, the gospel is essential. It is the starting point, and provides the basic foundation for life. Other material may be useful, after the gospel is firmly known and loved. Note though, nothing aids the soul until the gospel first makes way for support.

In these pages, you will find reflections on the rejuvenating power of the gospel taken from 2 Timothy 1:3-14. Paul writes this penetrating summary of the gospel to a young pastor — Timothy — whose fire is just about out. His confidence is low, and his courage has all but evaporated. He needs help, desperately. Knowing this, Paul invites him back to the garden of grace we know as the gospel.

David understood the same thing. He cried out to the Lord from the ends of the earth, because he understood his only secure and constant refuge was in the Lord.

Father, when my heart grows faint from the chaos and circumstance of this world, hear my cry, for you have been my refuge, and I need your strength to get up and walk worthy of your Son and my Savior, Jesus Christ, Amen.

CALL ME TO REMEMBER MY JESUS
DAVID W. HEGG

When, in a world gone mad, My Friend, you notice
my heart grown cold.
And the pleasures and pains of this temporal quest
Have stopped me from running, enamored with rest.
O then be to me a voice true and blessed;
Call me to remember my Jesus.

Though so expected, so few understood the place
of history's Event.
While the glory of God to man did appear,
The townsfolk were numb to the happenings there,
And at every door the message was clear:
"We have no room now for Jesus."

He came uninvited, or so it seemed. Few even knew
who He was.
But the way that He loved those of the Fall
And His trumpeting offer of deliverance to all,
Must be to my ears a clarion call
To imitate my Lord Jesus.

He came not for comfort, all must admit. The stable says it all.
So when my life from hardship is free
And my goal-setting sheet is crafted to be
A display of my longings, O Friend, challenge me
To magnify my Lord Jesus.

He came to His own, and they turned away.
Yet He continued pursuit.
Not mocking, nor hatred; not scourging, not pain
Did keep Him from Golgatha, His message plain

That all who would labor to seek sinners' gain
Must die to proclaim the Lord Jesus.

So what must I do? Where must I aim? To whom
shall my heart run?
For surely the age would fill up my thoughts
Regaling the "get to's", expunging the "oughts".
Yet I must remember my grace-cleansed spots,
And commune with my Lord Jesus.

"No room for Him here." What will I say, to people
so pleased in their doubt?
For surely my words will offer no light,
And my hands no care to those without sight,
Til my being is formed by that Bethlehem night,
And I come to reflect my Lord Jesus.

Thus, His truth is mine; so it must be. His life
my model, my word.
For though mankind's circumstances seem changed,
And scholars have the truth rearranged,
My message is decreed, though some find it strange.
I must witness of my Lord Jesus.

So Friend, be a Friend. Tell me the truth. Touch my
page with your pen.
And when I become distressed, overwrought,
When challenge and pain overwhelm
God-thought,
Remind me that He my freedom has
bought.
Call me to remember my Jesus.

1

WAKING UP IN ANCIENT EPHESUS

¹Paul, an apostle of Christ Jesus by the will of God according to the promise of the life that is in Christ Jesus, ²To Timothy, my beloved child: Grace, mercy, and peace from God the Father and Christ Jesus our Lord. ³I thank God whom I serve, as did my ancestors, with a clear conscience, as I remember you constantly in my prayers night and day. ⁴As I remember your tears, I long to see you that I may be filled with joy. ⁵I am reminded of your sincere faith, a faith that dwelt first in your grandmother Lois and your mother Eunice and now, I am sure, dwells in you as well. (2 Timothy 1:1–5)

If you are like me, the troubles of life often get you down. Things break. Plans go awry. Expectations go unmet, promises unfulfilled. Pressure mounts, obstacles form, criticism rises, and friends turn away. That is just in an average month!

When we look around at the world we live in, it just seems like things are not quite right. Bad guys do finish first, cheaters do prosper, and crime does pay. While we are straining to live righteously, humbly, and courageously for Christ, those sinners seem to be getting the biggest piece of the pie.

I can resonate with Jeremiah who cried *"Righteous are you, O LORD, when I complain to you; yet I would plead my case before you. Why does the way of the wicked prosper? Why do all who are treacherous thrive?"* (Jeremiah 12:1)

Asaph seems to understand when, in Psalm 73:3–9 he says:

> ³For I was envious of the arrogant when I saw the prosperity of the wicked. ⁴For they have no pangs until death; their bodies are fat and sleek. ⁵They are not in trouble as others are; they are not stricken like the rest of mankind. ⁶Therefore pride is their necklace; violence covers them as a garment. ⁷Their eyes swell out through fatness; their hearts overflow with follies. ⁸They scoff and speak with malice; loftily they threaten oppression. ⁹They set their mouths against the heavens, and their tongue struts through the earth.

But all these disappointments pale in comparison to those times we hit the wall of adversity, and begin to wonder if it is worth the cost to be salt and light in this broken world. Asaph's emotions mirror ours, as he described them in Psalm 73:12–14:

> ¹²"Behold, these are the wicked; always at ease, they increase in riches. ¹³All in vain have I kept my heart clean and washed my hands in innocence. ¹⁴For all the day long I have been stricken and rebuked every morning."

Have you ever been there? I have, and I am certain every Christ-follower can identify with these feelings.

Let us face the facts. There are times when our hearts grow faint, and we feel as though the race we have been called to run is too long, too strenuous, and will demand more of us than we can give. Just know, we are not the only ones.

Down through history many of God's people have understood those times when courageous hearts turned to jelly, and despite all they knew to be true of their God, they felt flattened by circumstance and despair.

Imagine waking up in ancient Ephesus to the sound of someone knocking at the door. *"Pastor Timothy, I have come from Paul with a letter to you!"*

Can you see Timothy stumbling to the door just as the night was giving way to morning? There he found a messenger holding a rolled parchment scroll from his mentor, the Apostle Paul. As he began to read, he realized Paul must have heard about his ongoing bout of spiritual discouragement. Now he was even more discouraged! How humiliating, to be left in Ephesus with such great responsibility and high hopes only to have those hopes dashed on the rocks of circumstance.

Timothy was certainly familiar with the malaise of spiritual fatigue and circumstantial adversity. Despite his lofty beginnings, he hit the wall and needed help from Paul himself. Timothy had it all going for him, and yet he was not immune to the struggles of living for Christ in the midst of a broken world.

For Timothy, ministry started with a providential meeting in his hometown. When it came to mentors, Timothy was blessed. During the time the Apostle Paul visited the little cluster of cities around Lystra, Timothy must have made quite an impression on him. After all, he came from a great family and had an impressive reputation.

Being the son of a Jewish mother and a Greek father, Timothy had the best of both worlds. The faith of his grandmother and mother had been passed down to him and was made real in his own life through his reading of the Scriptures. Apparently, Paul recognized in young Timothy a lofty spirituality and great potential for the Kingdom. He prevailed upon the family to let Timothy join his missionary team. Therein, Timothy must have become a trustworthy proclaimer and defender of the truth for Paul sent him on several significant missions, to Corinth, Philippi, and Thessalonica. Timothy was the great Apostle's choice to teach, encourage, and strengthen the churches during his missions.

While Timothy was still young by the standards of those days, Paul decided to leave him in Ephesus. He was instructed to help form and lead the fledgling gathering of Christ-followers. Timothy was to pastor the flock, teaching and modeling the truth of Scripture, as well as, correct those who were holding and promoting false doctrines. Paul wanted Timothy to be valiant for the truth in the midst of pagan Ephesus!

Paul's first letter to Timothy follows this theme of upholding, proclaiming, and defending the truth. His instructions are bookended between the charge to correct false teachers (1:3) and the command to preach the Word (4:1ff). Along the way, Paul reminds Timothy the church is the "pillar and support of the truth" (3:15). Timothy's first few years were all about the truth. This is certainly an essential for any ministry that intends to be true to Jesus Christ.

Over time, we come to find there are many other elements in living out the call of God on our lives. While the proclamation and defense of the truth are primary, foundational, and essential, the consequences of such a gospel-compelled life can be overwhelming. Those called to be God's spokesmen face the opposition of culture in every age, and it can be quite daunting.

Paul's second letter seems aimed at a discouraged, overwhelmed pastor who now understands the pressures and pitfalls of proclaiming the importance of living out the truth. It is clear this young pastor had hit the wall. Timothy certainly started out with a passion to preach, teach, and model the truth. After all, he was a Pauline protégée and had learned the ropes of ministry from the Apostle himself. But five years later, when Paul writes 2 Timothy, this young pastor is in a dire situation.

You do not have to be a pastoral professional to find encouragement in Paul's writing to Timothy. Every believer is called to be valiant for the truth of God, being a witness with both life and lip. It is no easy task. You do not have to be a church leader like Timothy to know this world is no friend to the law and counsel of God. Neither are the plans and pleasures of fallen society comfortable companions to the redeemed life. This world hated our Lord, and he said they would hate us too, as we reflect who he was and what he taught. Spiritual fatigue and evangelistic reticence are not temptations found only among pastors. We all feel them. We all know what it is like to go through periods of spiritual numbness or coldness or worse. Living a life that is conspicuously like Jesus is just plain hard.

We are going to see Timothy, for all his talent and youthful vigor, had been battered around by the culture of Ephesus. His energy and courage drained away by a five-year battle with circumstance. Paul now recognizes he must provide the advice and reflection necessary to rejuvenate this pastor's heart.

The question: What should Paul do to help Timothy? Paul's choice of subject and words may surprise you. Imagine someone you love has fallen into spiritual despondency. Maybe life had been rough for some time and there is no rest in sight. Imagine they come to you for some counsel and spiritual encouragement. What would you tell them?

I expect you might remind them of God's love, of the faithfulness he has shown to them in the past. You might suggest they take a vacation, or read a book you have found helpful in the past. Certainly, you would pray for, and with them, and promise to be on their side as they walked down the difficult path ahead.

Now think about Pastor Timothy. If I had been in Paul's shoes, I might have suggested he take a vacation, or ask for a Sabbatical. I might have given him the names of some retreat centers that specialize in helping burned out pastors, suggested a Eugene Petersen book, or even provided the means necessary for he and his wife to get away for a few days.

Paul surprises us! Rather than deal with the symptoms of fatigue, reticence, and fear, Paul goes to the heart of the matter. He gives Timothy a short course on the gospel.

Surely, Timothy — Pastor Timothy — would have been an expert in the subject. Was it not his job to know and preach the gospel story of God's great rescue mission in Christ? Why would Paul start reviewing the gospel with him?

The simple answer is we all need to reflect on, and rest in, the gospel every day. For years, we have thought of the gospel as simply the truth we believe to get into the family of God. And, so it is. However, it is much more than that. The gospel of Jesus Christ — the biblical story of God's sovereign love, and gracious redemption of sinners through faith in his son — is meant to be the foundation of our lives. The gospel reminds us daily that we are sinful, and causes us to say, in the words of the old hymn, *I need thee, O I need thee! Every hour I need thee.* In this way, the gospel humbles us under the mighty hand of God.

The gospel also reminds us our sin has been fully covered, paid for, and forgiven. The gospel comes into our darkest times of self-loathing and regret and declares we are righteous in Christ. It re-focuses our lives on the promises of God rather than on the defeats we suffer, and causes us once again to find refuge and rest under the wings of the Almighty.

That is what this book is all about and nothing more. It is an attempt, along with Paul, to remind you the gospel is a treasure to be enjoyed every day, no matter how many years you have walked with God.

The gospel is not now, nor has it ever been, the minimum amount of truth we must believe to gain heaven. Rather, it is the story of God's all-encompassing sovereign grace by which we have been redeemed, and in which we stand.

It is important to see where Paul begins. Before speaking directly to Timothy's malaise, he reminds him of his foundation. Notice Paul calls him "my true son" and goes on to highlight the fact Timothy's faith in Christ was not in question.

Two truths must be remembered when we fall into spiritual despondency, or try to help someone already there.

1. RELATIONSHIP MATTERS:

Paul loved Timothy. They had lived life together, walking side by side in the spiritual battle. If anyone had standing in Timothy's life, standing to call him to sober reflection on the gospel and encourage him to get back in the battle, it was Paul.

There is a lesson here. When I was a young pastor someone told me, *"No one will care what you know until they know that you care."* At the time, I scoffed at the idea, and chalked it up as one more sentimental "bumper sticker" cliché. Over the years, I have had to admit the truth and impact of that statement.

Paul cared about Timothy, and did so from a foundation of vital, trusted relationship. He had the right to confront Timothy and the character through which he not only would be heard, but his words accepted. Relationship can do that. Where love abounds, trust is built, and truth can be heard, even when it stings.

One of the devastating effects of spiritual fatigue is the tendency to isolate oneself from the very things and people we most need to help us to recover our spiritual equilibrium. Fortunately, if we are in a church family, there will be those who will reach out to us and refuse to let us be dissolved by our self-pity. We need this kind of friend, and all the more when the clouds of discouragement settle in around us.

We also need to be this kind of friend. Someone has said, *"True friends are the ones walking in when everyone else is walking out."* Even as we admit following Christ in this world will mean battling through adversity, we must also recognize God's plan for us is to be mutually dependent on, accountable to, and responsible for one another.

Paul's words to Timothy flow from a life-on-life friendship, grounded in their mutual love for Christ and dedication to his mission, and it is crucial for Christ-followers to follow his example today. We desperately need one another, especially when hearts grow faint.

2. REGENERATION MATTERS:

Paul began his encouragement of Timothy knowing that his friend was spiritually despondent, not spiritually dead. His young friend's faith had been tested over time, and found to be valid. There was no question the faith so clearly demonstrated in the lives of his mother and grandmother was alive in him as well.

This is so important. Many today struggle in their attempts to follow Christ and walk in holiness knowing they are attempting the impossible. They are trying to live the Christian life without Christ. It may even be the adversity they are experiencing is God's way of penetrating their hypocritical heart with a powerful message: *"You are still in bondage to sin, and no amount of religious ritual or wishful thinking can change that! Only a denial of self, coupled with the willingness to identify completely with Jesus, can fit you to follow him!"*

Before we go any further, let me ask you: Are you a Christ-follower? I am not asking if you go to church although you certainly should be part of a church family where the Bible is taught and modeled consistently. I am also not asking if you have made some verbal commitment to Jesus. I am asking if you are intentionally living your life in obedience to God's Word in the Bible because you have staked your eternal wellbeing on the promises that God has made to you in Jesus Christ. If you have, then this book may really help you wade through the valley of despair and come out the other side.

In addition, if you are still considering the claims of God and his promises in Christ, then this book will be a great help to you since it will explain simply and clearly the good news of God's forgiving grace extended to all mankind in the person and work of Jesus Christ.

With all this in mind, it is time to travel back to ancient Ephesus and meet Pastor Timothy.

2

**LOOKOUT FOR
BURNOUT**

[4]As I remember your tears, I long to see you, that I may be filled with joy. [5]I am reminded of your sincere faith, a faith that dwelt first in your grandmother Lois and your mother Eunice and now, I am sure, dwells in you as well. [6]For this reason I remind you to *fan into flame the gift of God*, which is in you through the laying on of my hands, [7]for God gave us a spirit not of fear but of power and love and self-control. [8]Therefore, do not be ashamed of the testimony about our Lord, nor of me his prisoner, but share in suffering for the gospel by the power of God,

(2 Timothy 1:4–8)

Chances are, if you attended college and enjoyed your academic journey, there was one special professor whose investment in your life continues to resonate in you today. In my case, it was John Sailhammer, whose willingness to eat lunch with a cocky sophomore was used of God to turn my heart and life direction 180 degrees. His classes were amazing, but lunch conversation is what I most remember and prized.

Paul and Timothy had that kind of relationship. Paul the mentor had poured his life into young Timothy and watched him grow into a man God could use to preach and teach and lead the church in Ephesus.

As we have seen, Paul recognized Timothy's deep faith, and loved him dearly. Paul was more than a great friend. He was also an apostle whose charge from Jesus himself gave him the authority to direct, encourage and confront those called to lead the flock of God. Timothy was one of those, and Paul recognized a deficiency in him that demanded correction. Before Paul gets to the cure — the gospel — he first has to diagnose and describe the condition adversely affecting both Timothy's heart and ministry.

Having expressed his deep conviction concerning Timothy's faith (vs. 5) he moves on to the first of four deficiencies he sees in Timothy. Combined together they have so debilitated Timothy that the ministry entrusted to him is in deep trouble.

In Paul's estimation, Timothy was almost burned out (vs. 6), increasingly fearful and timid (vs. 7), regularly acting as though he was ashamed of the gospel, (vs. 8a) and apparently paralyzed at the thought of suffering (vs. 8b). As we work through these, we will see that they are sequential, with each being the consequence of the one prior.

Timothy was near burnout because fear had sapped his courage, leaving him mired in timidity. This attitude of timidity arose out of a misplaced caution that to Paul looked as though Timothy was ashamed of him and the message of Jesus. At the root of it all appears to be a deep-seated reluctance to endure suffering for the name of Christ.

The illustration Paul uses to describe Timothy's condition plays well today. We are all aware of burnout, that emotional and physical state where nothing seems worth the effort of rolling out of bed.

In Timothy's case, the fire was his calling, his ministry, the position he now occupied in Ephesus, and the flame nearly extinguished. What this meant specifically in his case is impossible to tell. We can imagine his passion had waned significantly, and his efforts to bring the truth of God to bear on the people of Ephesus drastically curtailed.

Timothy had begun well, and the church had confirmed his calling to pastoral ministry. He exhibited both great gifts and great zeal, relishing the opportunity to set the fledgling church in Ephesus on the right foundation. Yet, whatever passion had filled his heart in the beginning was ready to die out. Paul had to remind him that the fire needed to be fanned back into flame.

The allusion to fire here simply means the flame of his calling to a pastoral position had gone from a robust blaze to flickering flame to embers with only the barest signs of heat. The fire was in danger of extinction, and urgency was required.

Timothy had been called by God and affirmed as a pastor by the presbytery and Paul himself. Through the symbolic laying on of hands, the church was affirming that God himself had laid his hand on Timothy and separated him for the work of pastoring.

Paul knew what he was doing in bringing up the "laying on of hands." He was reminding Timothy that the position he held, and the ministry demanded of it, was God's idea and not his. God had drafted Timothy and put him to work shepherding his flock.

If you are like me, you have suffered through times when the complexity of life and adverse circumstances in particular, seem overwhelming. Things that used to excite you no longer seem to matter at all. Perhaps that was what Timothy was feeling although we cannot know for sure. What we do know is the reality of burnout is no stranger to us today. As we may understand what it feels like, we are often unaware of its cause.

Paul's reminder to Timothy that God himself had placed him in Ephesus with a vital mission was the apostle's way of calling Timothy back to his essential identity. At some point Timothy had forgotten who he was, and more importantly, whose he was. His decisions and actions were being directed, not by a deeply felt conviction that obedience to God was always his best option, but by the felt needs of the moment. Rather than rest in the security of God's sovereign love and omniscient determination of all things, Timothy was giving in to the temptations we all face when things are not going our way. At some point, he started looking out for his own interests rather than surrender them to God as a prerequisite to magnifying his glory and accomplishing his plan.

It is no different for us today. The most prominent cause of burnout in the lives of Christ-followers is failure to own our essential identity every day, and order our lives accordingly.

As Christ-followers our essential identity is bound up in three things:

1) Who our God is; 2) Who God has made us to be in Christ; and 3) What God has called us to in the world.

Let us look at each of these carefully.

1. WHO OUR GOD IS

A. W. Tozer said, "*What comes into your mind when you think of God is the most important thing about you.*" Unfortunately, knowledge of God is often an area where we are quite deficient these days. Yes, we can say he is loving, and kind, and certainly able to hear and answer our prayers. However, when it comes to really understanding his nature, his attributes, and his eternal plan, we are too often just nibbling around the edges.

What do we need to remember about our God when our hearts grow faint? God is sovereign. God is faithful. He is our only hope in this life and the next. These simple facts, if properly understood, can get you through every circumstance that comes your way in this cruel world.

To say God is sovereign is simply to acknowledge that he does all he pleases, is never curtailed by anything, and all he does is best and right. How could it be otherwise? As God he cannot be less than perfect in all his ways or less than right in all his decisions. This being true, God's sovereignty becomes the greatest refuge ever.

At times, the issue of God's sovereignty hits us sideways, as though it puts us in dangerous territory. This is only because we have no human models of this kind of sovereignty. Lord Acton gave us his maxim, and it has stuck in our minds. *"Power corrupts, and absolute power tends to corrupt absolutely."* Consequently, we are wary of ceding to God anything like absolute power.

I want you to consider another point. God is also infinite, in that nothing about him is limited. He is not limited as to time or space. On the other hand, he is also not limited in terms of goodness, knowledge, or love. Think of it! God is infinite in his love, infinite in his goodness, knowledge, compassion, holiness, and power. Moreover, if this is true, then God's infinite power is always aligned with his infinite goodness. His infinite holiness is never contrary to his infinite love. Therefore, not only does he accomplish all he intends to do, but also everything he does is always best and right.

Let me add one more thing here. This God of the infinite is our God. In Christ, we find him to be our eternal Father, whose love will never leave us, and whose promise to make us increasingly more like Christ will absolutely be accomplished.

Do you see the importance of this? It means in every circumstance, God is always our best option. Whether our circumstances are wonderful or horrible, God is always our refuge, our strength, our protector, and provider. It also means recognizing our identity as fundamentally shaped by his love and truth is the safest way to start and end each new day.

Secondly, this sovereign God can be trusted. My kids will read this last statement and say "well duh!" And I agree it probably goes without saying that the God who only does what is best and right can be trusted at all times.

However, if you are like me, there can be an emotionally created gap between my mind and my heart. There can be a sizable canyon between my theological convictions and the stressed out wondering of my troubled heart. At times, the things I am feeling seem to overwhelm the things I know. I need to be reminded the God of my theology is also the Shepherd of my soul. He is sovereign, and he trustworthy, and he is mine. The added bonus: if you are in Christ, he is yours as well!

Lastly, this sovereign God who is infinitely trustworthy is our only hope in this life and the next. That just makes plain sense does it not? Why would we look elsewhere for purpose and satisfaction? If we place our hope ultimately in anything within the reach of this world's brokenness eventually we will be sorely disappointed. In fact, that is what usually brings on our discouragement. We hitch the wagon of our wellbeing to the horses of this fallen world only to be disappointed, and then wonder why our hearts are discouraged and growing faint.

Our identity as Christ-followers must start with a consistent and reverent recognition that the Almighty is our God and Father. Consequently, in every situation he is working to bring about the very best for us when measured against his divine purposes. All God brings into our lives is always best if we believe the purpose of our lives is to bring him glory.

This sentiment is beautifully captured in the Heidelberg Catechism, Q & A #26:

> Q. What do you believe when you say, "I believe in God, the Father almighty, creator of heaven and earth?"

A. That the eternal Father of our Lord Jesus Christ, who out of nothing created heaven and earth and everything in them, who still upholds and rules them by his eternal counsel and providence, is my God and Father because of Christ the Son.

I trust God so much that I do not doubt he will provide whatever I need for body and soul, and will turn to my good whatever adversity he sends upon me in this sad world.

God is able to do this because he is almighty God. He desires to do this because he is a faithful Father.

2. WHO GOD HAS MADE US TO BE IN CHRIST

Our identity as Christ-followers flows out of the nature, attributes, and plan of Almighty God. It is found most prominently in who he has made us to be in Christ.

Throughout his writings Paul refers to the believer in Jesus as being "in Christ." Our identity is no longer found "in sin" because we have been rescued from the domain of darkness and transferred to the kingdom of Jesus Christ. If anyone looks for us, they will find us "in Christ." This may seem like a strange way to picture our relationship yet it beautifully images the spiritual connection we have with our God and Savior.

One of the most exciting truths about every Christ-follower is they have been brought back into a profound union with God. In concise words, the fracture created by Adam's sin has been completely healed. Those once alienated and estranged have been reconciled. The lost have been found, the dead brought back to life, and enemies have been adopted into the family as beloved sons and daughters. Repeatedly in Scripture, this truth is both proclaimed and illustrated, and it speaks directly to the heart of every Christ-follower's essential identity.

We are more than just found, reconciled, reborn sons and daughters. According to Paul, we are the masterworks through whom God, the Master Craftsman, is intending to show off the greatness of his glory.

In Ephesians 2:1–10 Paul traces every Christ-follower's journey. We began in the realm of spiritual death, in which we walked in step with the wickedness that permeates our fallen world. God could have left us in that state, but his relentless love drove him to make us alive through the redemptive work of Jesus Christ. The apostle assures us that this spiritual rebirth was in no way accomplished by our work. On the contrary, our very existence as redeemed and reformed children of God is His work. In fact, he intends the exquisite craftsmanship of our existence to exalt his splendor. We are his samples, the great demonstration pieces through which the glories of his grace will shine for all eternity.

What a privilege is ours, to be the means by which the exquisite abilities of our God are advertised before a watching world. This is our identity. This is who we are, by God's grace, and this is where we will always find our greatest comfort, security, and satisfaction.

It is here we face one of the most crucial dilemmas of our time. We know we are "in Christ" as billboards of his grace and truth yet we too often seek to find our identity elsewhere. We turn from the privilege of being the masterwork of God, to shine our own light by different means.

Think about it. We foolishly attempt to establish our identity through our careers, our possessions, or even our families. We seek to "find ourselves" in our education, our writing, even our preaching. It is all too easy today to define success in ways that actually distance us from our truest identity as servants of Christ. And the further we move away from who we really are, the more susceptible we will be to the discouragement and despair this world throws at us.

This is not at all to say our work, families, education, or other noble pursuits are without merit. They certainly are! However, when our dedication to any of them eclipses our delight in Christ and his mission, we have begun the slow and dangerous slide away from who we truly are. In addition, if we do not put the brakes on, we will end up wondering why life just does not seem satisfying any more. As children of God, we have a new spiritual DNA, and the stuff of this world will not satisfy any more. We have been re-born for something far greater.

3. WHAT HE HAS CALLED US TO IN THE WORLD

The final piece in every Christ-follower's identity is the mission to which we all have been called, the "something greater" for which we have been given new life in Christ. Our God is sovereign, trustworthy, and our only hope. He has rescued and re-created us in Christ so that we are now representations of what his transforming grace can do to a life, and to a group of lives called the church.

The big question still remains: *Did God save us for ourselves? Or, did he save us for himself?*

It is easy today, in our consumer driven world, to buy into the self-centered fairy tale that everything exists for us. The advertising world screams it with their never ending message that we deserve the best, need the best, and must have the best … because we are the best! We are exhorted to look out for our best interests, demand our rights, and bellow our outrage if anyone dare violate them. We have become a society of spoiled brats, living each day to maintain this selfish title. Sadly, the church is dying as a result.

Here is the deal. God did not save us so we could feel good. He saved us so he could look good. By this, I do not intend to imply God ever looks bad. On the contrary, he has created all things for his glory, and intends them to be instruments of his majesty.

In our case, though created as God's image, sin profoundly corrupted our ability to reflect the glory of God. Simply put, God's redemptive activity in our lives restores our capacity to participate in the grand symphony of creation whereby the song of our creator's magnificence is being played.

Yet, in every Christ-follower there remains a strain of pride that can easily assume God's rescue was only intended for their personal enrichment, and eternal wellbeing. This is both selfish and downright sad. God did not purchase our redemption, and grant us a place in his family just so we could feel good. His purpose was to redeem and reform us so that his glory — his goodness! — would be seen in and through our transformed lives.

We are his samples, his show-off pieces, and his billboards, remember? Here is the grand fact that those who delight in Christ have come to know and treasure. When God looks the best in and through us that is when we will feel the best in him. John Piper said it best. *"We will be most satisfied when God is most glorified."*

When it comes to our essential identity, we will grasp it most when we are serving the mission of Christ consistently. That is, when we see our lives as engaged in the greatest rescue mission ever, partnering with Jesus Christ in the rescue and reformation of those still dead in sin and heading for eternal judgment.

What does this engagement look like? It is not what you might think if you imagine evangelism as pouncing on unsuspecting people with an unfamiliar message, centered on an unbelievable story, about an unusual man, who lived centuries ago. All that does is make them uncomfortable and you unwilling to do it too often.

The mission of Christ is not something we do outside of who he has made us to be and where he has placed us in this world. Being a "missionary" is simply living on mission in the everyday rhythms of life. Being an "everyday evangelist" is taking the gospel with you everywhere, wearing it with courage and kindness, as you share the story of God's transforming grace and truth with both life and lips.

I have found the greatest reason we are not more engaged in everyday evangelism is simply unbelief. It is not unbelief in Jesus or the power of the gospel. Rather, it is unbelief that those around us — our neighbors, the guy you coach beside, and the people at the gym — desire to engage in meaningful relationships and conversations with us. If God is drawing them to Jesus, it just could be they are ready to take advantage of any opportunity to scratch the itch he is causing in their minds and hearts.

God calls all of us to bloom where he has planted us, to shine where he has installed us, and to witness in the world where, in his providence, he has put us. Each of us has been placed in the middle of a whole network of people. Everyone we meet either is a Christ-follower, or needs to be. If we believe God is still drawing people to Jesus, then it is our privilege to partner with him, through the gospel, in this great redemptive adventure. It is, after all, who we really are.

Timothy had been called of God and affirmed by the church to pastor in Ephesus. Somewhere along the way, the flame of his passion began to die down and now was almost out. He was suffering from burnout, and Paul knew just where to direct him.

If we look closely, we can see Timothy had wandered away from his essential identity as evidenced by these three things. First, he had stopped being amazed by the sovereign, faithful God who had graciously rescued him from the brokenness of sin, drafted him for pastoral service, and designed him with the necessary gifts to accomplish the mission. Apparently, Timothy no longer lived each day in awe of his God and his calling.

Secondly, due to his lack of awe, he had begun wondering if God could actually be trusted to keep the promises, he had made to him in Christ.

Thirdly, the result was a diminished desire to be involved in the mission of Christ, especially, as we will see, if it meant he might have to suffer.

We can all identify with Timothy in this. It is far too easy to lose our daily awe of God and begin to wonder if he still cares for us, especially when life throws adversity at us. Perhaps the problem stems from the fact that we have expended so much energy trying to live for God that we have forgotten the joy of living with him, as the foundation of who we really are. It is our privilege to dwell with God, to live in wonder of his sovereign love so brilliantly extended to us in the gospel of Jesus Christ. We will never burnout if we endeavor to dwell near the great flame of God's glory.

3

• • • ▬ ▬

FEARING FEAR
ITSELF

[4]As I remember your tears, I long to see you, that I may be filled with joy. [5]I am reminded of your sincere faith, a faith that dwelt first in your grandmother Lois and your mother Eunice and now, I am sure, dwells in you as well. [6]For this reason I remind you to fan into flame the gift of God, which is in you through the laying on of my hands, [7]for *God gave us a spirit not of fear but of power and love and self-control*. [8]Therefore, do not be ashamed of the testimony about our Lord, nor of me his prisoner, but share in suffering for the gospel by the power of God,
(2 Timothy 1:4–8)

Paul begins now to probe further into the reasons behind Timothy's condition. Moreover, he does not have far to look. In verse 7 Paul puts his finger on a serious flaw in his younger partner. He is very direct. *God has not given you this spirit of fear!*

Before going any further it is necessary to identify just what this "fear" is, and what it is not. Throughout the Bible, we are called to "fear God." In fact, fearing God is one of the essential characteristics of the righteous man or woman. Those who do not fear God are counted as enemies of God.

Fear of God is a deep recognition of God's exalted position and his sovereign right to rule all creation as best pleases him. This fear inspires awe, compels reverence and worship, and motivates obedience. All of these are good fruits of a proper fear of God. We desire to please him, and fear disappointing or disobeying him.

Paul is clear that the "spirit of fear" Timothy has adopted is not pleasing to God. Rather, it is an obstacle to truly fearing God and living obediently before him. It is an ungodly fear, an unhealthy fear, and one that threatens Timothy's very life and ministry.

We are not told just how Paul came to know so much about Timothy's pastoral downgrade, but it is clear that Timothy was exhibiting traits unbecoming to a pastor. Chief among these was this growing sense of fear. An even better description would be timidity. His spiritual fatigue and lethargy — his burnout — were only the latest consequences of a far greater problem. Timothy had developed a reticence Paul saw as potentially paralyzing, and in need of direct confrontation.

Timothy started out with a passion to proclaim and defend the truth. He entered into the pagan communities of Ephesus with confidence. Somewhere along the line, something happened.

Maybe the opposition of certain people had been too strong. Maybe some of his fellow Christ-followers had turned on him. Perhaps the false teachers were mighty in their teaching and arguments, and Timothy was not able to oppose them with confidence. We just do not know. What we do know is Timothy was no longer valiant for truth. He was back on his heels, shying away from the battle. He had adopted timidity as his preferred style.

It may even have been that Timothy considered this timidity more spiritually minded than his previous way of ministry. Perhaps he decided to "go along to get along." Maybe he had been too harsh and decided a more reserved, timid approach was best. Such a view is always popular, especially in our day. Whatever the case, Paul is quick to point out timidity is not what the Lord passes out as standard equipment to those he calls to join his family and bear the family crest. Timidity may appease the culture, but it does not please God.

Everything we could say about Timothy also applies to us today. We are all tempted to be timid. It is always easier to stay away and keep our mouths shut than it is to intentionally engage our world in the name of Christ. Yet, who are we kidding? Timidity has never been a spiritual gift.

Timidity grows out of the emotional soil of fear, and fear always seems to be lurking in the shadows of our lives, even as Christ-followers. Timothy certainly had his fears, as do you and I. Fear can be both demoralizing and debilitating. Fear can tie us up in knots and keep us from moving forward. It can also greatly diminish our ability to trust God passionately, consistently, and courageously.

At the risk of being redundant, it must be said again, most of the time fear grows strongest when our knowledge and awe of God cease to be front and center in our lives. The further we are away from delighting in the sovereignty and faithfulness of our God, the more susceptible we will be to fear the things of this world.

Fortunately, Paul does not leave Timothy or us hanging. While fear is an ever-present temptation given the state of our world, God has given us ways to overcome it, but we have to be active in this process. There is no such thing as "couch potato" Christianity. When it comes to overcoming fear we must be proactive, and take advantage of God's provision. He does not pass out fear as standard equipment for Christ-followers. Rather, Paul says he has given us *power, love, and self-control*. It is up to us to understand and employ them in the fight against fear.

We need to look at each of these, understanding they are all tools God grants his children to enable consistency and fervency in following Christ.

POWER

Our world is enamored with power. Businessmen wear power suits with power ties and schedule power lunches. We all munch on power bars, mock cars lacking power, and covet positions of power. You can even go to the App Store and find scores of free apps to increase the power of your speaking, writing, scheduling, efficiency, cooking, and any number of other areas of life that absolutely, positively just have to be more powerful if you are ever to compete in this world!

Power is a coveted commodity simply because weakness is so weak, or so our world believes. However, the Apostle Paul learned that God's power is perfected in our weakness.

In 2 Corinthians 12 he describes his "thorn in the flesh" experience when God humbled his pride. During this time of divinely imposed weakness God declared the Apostle's personal power could never stand up to the challenges facing him. Rather, he should rely on God's empowering grace and realize the paradoxical truth that the power of God is best experienced when wrapped around human weakness.

Of course, this does not mean we just sit back and become couch potato Christians. It does not mean we refuse to *run with endurance the race that is set before us*" (Heb. 12:1), "*work(ing) out (our) own salvation with fear and trembling*" (Phil 2:12). It does not mean we stop trying with all our might to accomplish the tasks God has assigned to us. It does demand we recognize and rest in the fact that it is God's power, working through us that accomplishes his will.

Paul understood this, and even put it down carefully for us in Colossians 1:28–29. After stating his great ambition to proclaim Christ in order to "*present everyone mature in Christ,*" he makes this amazing, essential point:

> "*For this I toil, struggling with all his energy that he powerfully works within me.*"

We need to unpack what Paul knew was so important in this sentence written to the Christ-followers in Colossae.

His dramatic statement is essential to our understanding of the relationship between the power of God and our attempts to live spiritually vital lives.

Notice first, Paul is working hard, even toiling, and struggling. He is running the race set before him, with perseverance and a desire to win. He is not looking for comfort or ease. He is in the battle, everyday, as God has called him to be.

But also notice he is depending completely on the energy of God powerfully working within him. God's power is being worked out through Paul's diligent toil and struggle. We could explain it this way:

Question: How does Paul know the power of God is working through him?

Answer: Paul knows the power of God is working through him when he is diligently toiling to accomplish the work God has given him to do ... according to God's power!

Lastly, we must understand just where the power of God resides. The power for anything God calls us to is found in the complementary ministries of the Word and the Spirit. The Spirit of God uses the word of God to do the work of God in and through the people of God. It is the Spirit working through the word, or we could say it is the word illumined and activated by the Spirit. Either way the result is the same. God's power, by which we are progressively matured personally, and enabled increasingly to live righteously and dynamically in this sin-drenched world, is to be found only in a consistent passion for Scripture coupled with a humble reliance on the Spirit.

In reality, the ministries of the Spirit and the Word form a self-perpetuating cycle in the lives of healthy, vital Christ-followers. A sincere desire to walk in the power of the Spirit will drive you to the Scriptures, for it is through the inspired, inerrant Word that the voice of God is heard. It is through the diligent study and understanding of God's Word, coupled with a radical determination to live obediently to its truths, that the power of the Spirit is manifested in real time. Therefore, the cycle goes. To walk in the Spirit we are driven to the Word, and to obey the Word we humbly depend on the Spirit. In this way, our diligent, humble obedience becomes the power of God through which his will is accomplished.

Apparently, Timothy had forgotten this somewhere along the line. Perhaps in the midst of discouragement or disappointment, he had wandered away from the soul-nourishing experience of time in God's Word. Perhaps his prayers had become both insipid and infrequent. Perhaps the pace and challenge of ministry had him believing he did not have time to feed his own soul. It is impossible to tell just what started his descent away from a daily experience of union and communion with God, but it was evident to Paul that Timothy was experiencing a power outage. Whatever he was substituting for the power of the Spirit through the Word had no chance of succeeding. The mounting failure had him back on his heels.

LOVE

It is a magnificent comfort to know God has given us a spirit of love. That is, he has reconstituted us as objects, recipients, and containers of his love. His love has captured us, changed us, and now fills us, and we can never appreciate or marvel at this enough. To say God loves us is to say he has brought us into his love so that we can love as he loves.

The love we are to manifest in every place is love for God and man. To love God is supremely to desire him above all else, and obey him as the core principle of life. It is this love of God, enabling our love for God, that casts out fear (1 John 4:18). When we love God, as he deserves, marveling at his sovereignty, goodness, faithfulness, and power, we find the fear of this world minimized by comparison. What we have in God is so glorious that our earthly fears lose their power.

It seems Timothy had lost his zeal to love God and others rightly. Perhaps, he had become fixated on his own pain, his own unmet expectations. Whatever the reason, Paul feels compelled to remind him the correct attitude of love is something we receive from God, the giver of the greatest love of all. Timothy desperately needs an attitude adjustment.

When we lose our desire to love it usually stems from a selfish preoccupation with our own problems, our own hurt feelings, and our own overall wellbeing. The love of God, modeled in Jesus, and deposited in us to be worked out through us, is an external activity, always pointed outward to God and others. When turned inward, it fosters pride and selfishness. When these combine in our hearts our love is replaced with anger, pettiness, and a critical spirit, all of which foster deep frustration and discouragement. Remember, those who only find fault in others are seldom content in themselves.

SELF-CONTROL

Paul here directs Timothy to another aspect of God's redeeming grace. He has not given us a spirit of fear. Rather, he has granted us access to power through the Spirit and the word. Secondly, he has filled us with his love and enabled us to share it widely. Lastly, he has rescued our minds from the corruption of sin so that we can now exercise right thinking.

Self-control here, as used by Paul, is best understood as sound, disciplined judgment, or simply a "sound mind." As Christ-followers, we can now fill our minds with biblical truth, and grow in both knowledge and discernment, through the ministry of God the Spirit who dwells in us all. This discernment, then, can increasingly enable us to choose the best way to think, act, and react in this world. Paul put it this way:

> [9]"And it is my prayer that your love may abound more and more, with knowledge and all discernment, [10]so that you may approve what is excellent, and so be pure and blameless for the day of Christ ..."
> (Philippians 1:9–10).

Did you notice that the "sound mind" flows out of, and is a function of, the love of God and for God with which the Christ-follower has been filled by the Spirit of God? In addition, when this love abounds, discernment grows, better choices are made, and our lives are increasingly aligned with the grace and truth of Christ.

Timothy had fallen into fear, and it was paralyzing his effectiveness for the Savior. Just what he was afraid of is not clear at this point but perhaps Paul's call to embrace suffering gives us a clue. Was Timothy facing persecution? Were the Ephesians making his life hard? Perhaps. Whatever the case, his best option was never to give in to the fear and turn away from the ministry given him by God. Rather, his best option was to use the power, love, and self-control God had given him, and not stray far from the refuge God provided.

Today too many of us are also living in both fear and unbelief. We are hampered by our fears and we do not believe God can allay them. It may even be these fears are keeping us from fully enjoying our identity as Christ-followers. If so, what do we do?

We can do no better than understand what Paul told Timothy centuries ago. If our fears are keeping us from boldly living for Christ and witnessing of his grace and truth before a watching world, it is definitely time to exercise the power, love, and self-control God has granted to us in Jesus Christ.

It is time to engage our God through the power of the word and Spirit, be drawn deeper into the love God has for us, and begin strengthening and exercising the sound mind God enables in us through his truth and love.

4

• • • • —

THE SHAME OF
BEING ASHAMED

[4] As I remember your tears, I long to see you, that I may be filled with joy. [5] I am reminded of your sincere faith, a faith that dwelt first in your grandmother Lois and your mother Eunice and now, I am sure, dwells in you as well. [6] For this reason I remind you to fan into flame the gift of God, which is in you through the laying on of my hands, [7] for God gave us a spirit not of fear but of power and love and self-control. [8] *Therefore, do not be ashamed of the testimony about our Lord,* nor of me his prisoner, but share in suffering for the gospel by the power of God,
(2 Timothy 1:4–8)

Paul had directly diagnosed the first two complications in Timothy's spiritual health. His flame of desire and urgency for Christ had burned dangerously low. Added to that was a fear-driven timidity that had come to define his ministry activity. He was discouraged and back on his heels, and Paul was determined to confront those areas and help restore vitality in his pastoral partner.

There was still more diagnosing to do. The problems of burnout and timidity did not just spring up by themselves. They came from some other far deeper problem in Timothy's life.

In verse 8, Paul gets to the heart of the matter. Timothy's spiritual flame was just about out, and he had adopted a timid stance because, at the core of his being, he was ashamed of the very message he had been charged to carry. When Paul commands Timothy not to be ashamed of the testimony of the Lord, it can only mean that Paul believed this to be all too true in the life of the young pastor.

This shows us just how desperate the situation was for Timothy in Ephesus. Life was hard. Opposition was real, and despair was constant and overwhelming. Living out the gospel was hard work, and there seemed to be little, if any, reward for doing so.

Perhaps Timothy had begun shaving the edges from the gospel message. Maybe he had minimized the fact sin was real and carried an eternal sentence before the throne of heaven. Perhaps he was weary of hearing the mocking response of his Ephesian neighbors to the story of Jesus. We are not told. What we do see is Timothy's passion for the truth becoming so weak that, to the casual onlooker, it appeared he no longer championed the gospel. It looked as if he were ashamed of it.

Paul certainly understood the gospel could breed resentment even as it judges and critiques the sinful heart.

He had felt it himself. He knew the gospel story fell like the fragrance of death to many who heard it. He had written as much in 2 Corinthians 2:15–16:

> [15]For we are the aroma of Christ to God among those who are being saved and among those who are perishing, [16]to one a fragrance from death to death, to the other a fragrance from life to life. Who is sufficient for these things?

Paul knew the feelings of inadequacy in the face of gospel ministry. Perhaps Timothy was increasingly aware of his own inabilities. Perhaps the bloody story of the cross, or the truth of God's electing love, or the radical holiness pressed upon those who followed Christ were so hard to proclaim that Timothy was finding it easier to edit the gospel down to the parts that fell easily on the ears of his Ephesian neighbors.

Again, we do not know. What we do know is to be ashamed of the gospel is to entirely miss its point.

If Paul had felt as Timothy was feeling at some time in his life, he had also found the solution. While parts of the gospel story fell awkwardly on the hearts of the unbelieving, the whole story was their only hope. The gospel was God's saving power, and that certainly was nothing to cause shame. Paul wrote confidently of this to the Romans in 1:16–17:

> [16]For I am not ashamed of the gospel, for it is the power of God for salvation to everyone who believes, to the Jew first and also to the Greek. [17]For in it the righteousness of God is revealed from faith for faith, as it is written, "The righteous shall live by faith."

Certainly, Timothy was facing his own set of obstacles. As I look around, many Christians live as though they are ashamed of the testimony of Christ today. They are reluctant to live out its full demands, and hesitant to share the story with intentionality in the normal rhythms of life.

Today it is just too easy to become complacent about the gospel story, and especially the life it calls us to lead. After all, living righteously in an ungodly world is hard and it often asks more of us than we care to give. Face it, it is much easier to live the comfortable life of modern Christianity, rationalizing little compromises here and there, and considering church attendance, and occasional Bible reading as marks of maturity.

Deep down we know we are not satisfied. When we hear others speak about their intimacy with God, the delights they find in knowing and applying his word to their everyday lives, and the confidence they exude in trying times, it seems a bit foreign to our experience.

Perhaps some of this can be chalked up to the expectations we had when we first heard about Jesus. Maybe he was presented as the friend we needed, or the healer, or the rescuer, or better yet, the divine Life Coach offering to come alongside us and help us be super successful.

Chances are pretty good we were never called to acknowledge the vast ocean of sinfulness we knew lurked in our hearts much less the fact we deserved God's wrath. Jesus was presented as an "add on," as a new spiritual app designed to forgive our sins and make our lives all we could ever ask for.

The gospel, correctly understood and trusted, changes everything. It calls us away from the façade of religion to a soul-satisfying relationship with God the Father who has made himself known and accessible through Jesus Christ, God the Son. It is not so much that Jesus has come to us for our benefit. Rather, he has brought us to God the Father for his benefit, that we might be part of the great company of re-created people through whom his glory will shine eternally. Again, as John Piper has so aptly said, *"We will be most satisfied when God is most glorified."*

Timothy's fainting heart was a result of his turning away from what God called him to be and do. In turning away from God to satisfy his self, he was fleeing the only true source of satisfaction in this bad world.

Jesus stated it directly, *"And he said to all, "If anyone would come after me, let him deny himself and take up his cross daily and follow me."* (Luke 9:23)

Think for a moment about Jesus' first demand: *"let him deny himself …"* We too often think self-denial means pain, as in denying ourselves certain goodies when dieting, or certain purchases we know are not in the plan of good stewardship. It should be clear here Jesus would never demand something that was not ultimately the best option for us.

The self-denial he commands is simply the recognition certain of our desires and wants, dreams, impulses, and infatuations are actually harmful for us. When Jesus calls us to deny ourselves he is calling us away from the toxic desires of our sinful hearts and into the refuge of obedience to him. To deny self is simply to recognize all Jesus asks of us is always best for us. In addition, all he has for us is exemplified, advertised, imbibed, and enjoyed in the gospel.

In the popular game of Poker, there is a point in every match where one player decides to go "all in." He chooses to risk his remaining chips on the hand he holds. He will either win, or go down in flames and be out of the match. There are no second chances, no safety nets, and no ties.

Timothy's problem was he no longer felt "all in" for the gospel. His confidence in God, and zeal for ministry, had diminished to a dangerous level. At least it appeared that way from the manner of his life and witness. Where had the vitality and passion gone? What happened to the young man who was so valiant for truth, and ready to change the world? Where were his spiritual strength, his courage in the face of adversity, and his vigor for Christ?

In Timothy's example, we learn a very important truth that almost goes unrecognized in the church today. Those who attempt to follow Christ half-heartedly will ultimately be dissatisfied. The waves of trouble this world throws against our shores are relentless.

Day after day, when our expectations go unmet, our rights trampled on, or our sensitivities and preferences disregarded, we desperately need the strength that only comes from walking daily in obedience to Christ. Without Spirit-crafted, maturing character, we devolve into angry, critical, and sinful behaviors. We store up resentment, and call it righteous anger, and do it often enough that we rationalize our behavior as normal Christian living. Moreover, it does not matter how many years we boast of having walked with Jesus. For too many today, 20 years of following Christ has really been one year, 20 times. They have perfected the externals but deep down their hearts are faint when it comes to being "all in" for Christ.

I know because I have personally been there. We have all been there. The question is *will you be content to stay there*. What we need is a fresh, vital, and lasting appreciation of the gospel for what it really is and does. We will get there, but first we have one more of Paul's diagnoses concerning Timothy.

Through the lens of Timothy's life, we have looked at spiritual burnout, fear-driven timidity, and now a reluctance to be "all in" for Jesus. All these have their own consequences but in the next chapter, we finally get to the foul spring from which all these other bitter spiritual waters have been flowing. In Timothy's life, it was a debilitating unwillingness to suffer that brought on his spiritual fatigue and ministerial lethargy. Paul confronts him with the fact that following Jesus does not just demand we deny ourselves, but also that we intentionally and courageously take up the cross as those ready and willing to die.

5
• • • • •

SHARING IN SUFFERING

⁴As I remember your tears, I long to see you, that I may be filled with joy. ⁵I am reminded of your sincere faith, a faith that dwelt first in your grandmother Lois and your mother Eunice and now, I am sure, dwells in you as well. ⁶For this reason I remind you to fan into flame the gift of God, which is in you through the laying on of my hands, ⁷for God gave us a spirit not of fear but of power and love and self-control. Therefore, do not be ashamed of the testimony about our Lord, nor of me his prisoner, *but share in suffering for the gospel by the power of God,*
(2 Timothy 1:4–8)

The last thing on Paul's list as he writes to his friend, brother, and fellow-laborer in the church is his recognition that Timothy's timidity stemmed from his unwillingness to be faithful if it meant suffering. We finally have the full picture.

To the outside observer Timothy was showing signs of burnout. The flame was almost out. Fear-driven timidity had replaced vibrancy for Christ giving the impression, the young pastor was actually ashamed of the gospel. Tired and back on his heels, Timothy seemed content to be mediocre, to follow Christ, but at quite a distance. Now we know why. At the bottom of it all, was a life-dominating aversion to suffering.

Did he fear physical pain, or societal contempt, or other forms of opposition? Yes, most likely, just as we all do. Was it his discouragement and disappointment in ministry, combined with his growing reticence toward telling the gospel story that had him wondering if what he was called to was really worthy of suffering? Was he rationalizing the voice of compromise to actually be the voice of reason? After all, why suffer for the gospel if you can compromise just enough so your opponents accept you? Could not that be an appropriate philosophy of ministry?

Whatever the reason, Paul must call Timothy back to a fundamental truth. *Taking up the cross means identifying with those on their way to die.* Timothy needed to be recaptured by the call of Christ on his life, to own the mission of Christ as worth any amount of challenge and suffering presented in his life.

Paul believes in a "whatever it takes" ministry mentality knowing what God has for him through obedience is always his very best option. He also realizes the God who calls them to suffering always works through it for their good and his glory. First, Timothy must be led back to the core, back to the supremacy of the gospel.

If Paul knew what it was like to be a bit ashamed of the gospel, he also recognized such thinking would have devastating effects on the life and ministry of Timothy. The situation was dire. The man charged with proclaiming and defending the gospel in Ephesus was in trouble. He was near burnout. He was reticent, shying away from his challenges, and increasingly ashamed to be associated with the testimony of his Lord. He placed a higher value on his personal happiness than on fulfilling the mission of Christ.

In the West we know very little about suffering for the gospel, although recent events are causing us to consider what following Christ may mean for our families, churches, and Christian organizations. With religious freedom being redefined and potentially diminished, the reality of governmental persecution may be at hand.

Yet, it is not as though the western church is being spiritually powerful in the meantime. Even though we live in places where religious freedom is still our privilege, our influence is paltry. For the first time in history, those admitting no religious affinity outnumber the rest of us. If we are this weak without strong persecution, what will become of us when things really get tough?

The reality is we are just like Timothy. We are afraid to suffer for the gospel. We are even afraid of the potential of suffering, so much so we rarely wear Christ on our shirtsleeves, or speak of him among non-Christians. We are afraid of being rejected; afraid of being labeled; afraid of being considered less than cool, hip, "with it" or whatever other trendy descriptor you want to use. We are afraid someone might not like us, or worse, might argue with us in ways we cannot defend. We are afraid someone might think we are religious fanatics, or fundamentalists, or crazy, or politically "one of those." We are afraid of being marginalized, or mocked, or considered minimally intelligent. Face it, while we sing songs that shout our commitment to Christ as total and life-long, they are just songs, not reality.

At the foundation of this fear is an overwhelming sense of unbelief. Yes, unbelief. It is not unbelief in Christ, or the gospel but unbelief that God is still using the gospel to draw people to Jesus. It is unbelief that our neighbors, the regulars we know at the coffee shop, or the people we work with, are spiritually curious and hungry. It is unbelief that God the Spirit uses the gospel to open blind eyes and deaf ears, grant new life to sinners, and bring about true repentance and saving faith. All this unbelief stems from an insufficient recognition of the monumental truths that make up the gospel.

There is a direct connection between a deep appreciation for the doctrines that make up the gospel, and a courageous heart for Christ. This is why Paul exhorted Timothy to *share in suffering for the gospel by the power of God.* We are never called merely to suffer. Neither are we expected to endure suffering for the gospel apart from the power of God. And the power of God, as Paul will go on to show, springs from an everyday marveling and resting in what God has promised and Jesus Christ has accomplished in the truths that come together in the story we call the gospel.

As we will see, the gospel re-creates not only our lives, but also our whole perspective on life. It lifts our eyes from the temporal definitions of happiness and success to the infinite spiritual value of being "in Christ." It reminds us this life is merely the prelude to the next, and must be lived out in light of God's eternal promises. No matter your malady, confusion, fear, or dysfunction, the starting place of sorting it all out is a right understanding of, appreciation for, and faith-driven commitment to the truth of the gospel, and the demands it makes on your life.

When Christ-followers fail to grasp the vitality of the gospel daily, we slip into this compromised comfort of unbelief. We fail to honor, trust, and use the gospel as our sure guide for everyday living. Moreover, if this condition tarries, we follow Timothy's path to a reluctant life, timidity, and ultimately, a fainting heart.

We simply cannot forget Timothy was a pastor. While it may startle those in our congregations, we pastors must admit we have been in Timothy's shoes. I have felt this way myself. If you are a minister, laboring in the vineyard of God, you know the feeling as well. We have all been there ... burned out, timid, even toying with compromise. Maybe as you read this you are there now.

Sometimes loving Jesus Christ with an incorruptible love, living that love in conspicuous ways, and serving the flock of Christ seem like those dreams where we are running uphill against such a stiff wind we can hardly hold our own, much less make progress. Each day calls on us to fight the good fight. It never stops; it never relents. The call to deny self, shoulder the cross, and follow Jesus closely seems all too consuming. By this, I mean doing it well consumes our energy, our passion, our happiness, and our joy. It takes everything we have, and more often than not, we end up running on empty. Most importantly, we, the ones others look to for help, instruction and guidance, cannot afford to run on empty.

That is one of the many reasons I have written this little book. Too many of us — pastors, church leaders, and congregants alike — are trying to live, and love, and minister on empty. Yet, every day we drive by the waters of the gospel thinking we are just too busy to stop at that stream. My hope is, with Timothy, we will feel Paul pouring the refreshing, rejuvenating water of the gospel into our parched, tired souls.

Are you burned out? Has the race become too long and too grueling? Is your fuel gauge at the bottom? It is time to stop, rest, and take up the gospel. In it, you will find the power of God, the love of God, and the discipline necessary to stay in the race.

So, here we go …

6

— • • • •

THE GOSPEL
OF GOD

8Therefore do not be ashamed of the testimony about our Lord, nor of me his prisoner, but share in suffering for the gospel by the power of *God,* 9*who saved us* and called us to a holy calling, not because of our works but because of his own purpose and grace, which he gave us in Christ Jesus before the ages began, 10and which now has been manifested through the appearing of our Savior Christ Jesus, who abolished death and brought life and immortality to light through the gospel, 11for which I was appointed a preacher and apostle and teacher, 12which is why I suffer as I do. But I am not ashamed, for I know whom I have believed, and I am convinced that he is able to guard until that Day what has been entrusted to me.
(2 Timothy 1:8–12)

I have a friend named Kamil who is a noted orthopedic surgeon, and a passionate Christ-follower. He told me once about a conversation he had at a friend's dinner table. He and his family had been invited over for a relaxing Sunday afternoon meal, and as they sat down their host brought out a huge roast on a decorative platter. Looking at my surgeon friend, he asked, "Well Doctor, would you like to carve the roast?" Everyone chuckled until Kamil replied, "You know, anyone can cut it apart; the skill comes in putting it back together."

As a doctor, Kamil knew the most important component of his job was not the destructive part of the surgery, but the restorative part. Apparently, that was Paul's method as well. First, he diagnosed the problems in Timothy's life, and then he proceeded to apply the cure.

Timothy was engaged in ministry, and it was tough, much tougher than he thought it would be. The idolatrous culture of Ephesus was a constant force of opposition, and it appears Timothy's spiritual vitality was wasting away. He knew he was called to swim upstream against the current of culture, but the torrent was strong and the task was unrelenting. He needed rejuvenating. So what did Paul do? He gave him a short but substantial course in the gospel.

Today we might find this strange. Most of the time when Christ-followers encounter fears, spiritual fatigue, confusion, discouragement, or some other spiritual or emotional dysfunction, we point them to some good book, or a counselor, and maybe a vacation. At times, each of these can be an excellent resource. While other things may help after the heart is revitalized by the significance of the gospel, none will work apart from a gospel foundation first being laid.

The gospel begins with God. Paul declares it is God who has saved us and called us with a holy calling. This is so simple but so essential: God both begins and completes the work of salvation. God saves sinners. This essential starting point of the gospel story sets the course for the rest.

First, the gospel is all about God, not us. The power of the gospel is God, and the purpose of the gospel is his glory. Too often today the gospel story starts with a focus on the human need to find a better life. It moves on from there to assert God is waiting to give this life, along with many other benefits, if we will only let him. He is there, pleading for a chance to help us, to right the wrongs, break the addictions, forgive our past indiscretions, and see to it we begin living our best life now.

If this is the gospel then Paul really got it wrong. He tells Timothy the gospel story begins with God. He is the Savior, the rescuer, and the one who deserves the priority and all the glory. We were the ones in need of rescue, and the clear teaching of the Bible is, not only were we unable to effect our own rescue, we did not deserve God's attention at all. Our brokenness was due to our insistence on living life on our own terms, and the only thing God owed us was justice in the form of punishment for breaking his law.

Paul starts Timothy's spiritual therapy with a simple reminder that salvation is of the Lord, the same thing Jonah reluctantly realized in his waterfront room in the belly of the great fish. As much as we would like it to be, the gospel is not first about us; it is first about God. He is the author, and he decides what it is and how his plan will be accomplished. Jonah failed to recognize this important point. When God charged him with a preaching mission to pagan Nineveh, he balked. How dare God offer the grace of forgiveness and relationship to those Gentile heathen! Yet eventually he came to the truth: salvation, as well as the message that proclaims it, belongs to the Lord our God. It is, from first to last, from him, about him, and ultimately for him.

Let us hit the pause button here for just a minute. Before going on, it is important for us to grasp the practical ramifications of what I have just said. To say salvation is God's doing is not just some theological assertion although it is one of the most essential theological points the Bible makes. If we apply this truth to our personal situations, we will find something that can breathe contentment and vitality into our everyday lives.

Salvation was God's idea. Your salvation was God's idea. To bring you out of death into life demanded infinite wisdom, strength, knowledge, and love ... all combined into redemptive power God alone could wield. God has directed his sovereignty at you in the greatest rescue mission ever, and you have been the recipient of his grace. God's grace in your life changes everything. You are no longer who you were, for now you are a child of God, a citizen of the heavenly kingdom, a brother to Christ, and part of the most influential company ever known, the church.

That is correct. You are not alone. God's plan was never simply about individuals but about gathering a group, a holy nation, and a people that could be his own prized possession. You are part of a much larger plan than your own personal wellbeing. You are privileged to be part of his billion-pixel display on which the magnificence of his glory and the transforming power of his grace are being beamed around the world.

Through you and millions more, God is displaying his sovereignty over all things as well as his promise to ultimately set all things to rights. Through us, as messengers of the gospel, God is showing the world a power it cannot overcome, a sin it cannot deny, a love it cannot measure, and a salvation available to all who will humble themselves in true repentance and saving faith. Yes, dear Christ-follower, that is who you are, all because God set his love on you.

Therefore, salvation belongs to God. So, just what is it about God that forms the gospel? To simplify the gospel may always be to oversimplify the gospel. Certainly, we can summarize it if we are careful to include its essential parts and give them all the weight the Bible gives them.

There is no doubt the gospel story begins with God, who brought all things into being through his word. This word was his activity in creation, and the result was very good. That is, it was very good until sin came crashing in bringing corruption to every part of God's world. It is here the "bad news" of sin becomes the necessary backdrop against which the "good news" of the gospel can shine with eternal brilliance.

Sin, like a monstrous computer virus, invaded creation's operating system and began to replicate itself until it was pervasive in every nook and cranny. Nothing was outside its reach. The effect of sin's pervasive invasion was both corruption of all creation, and comprehensive human sinfulness. Death became normal. Decay was commonplace. All creation began to groan under the brokenness of sin's corrupting influence. Every system God had created was now polluted, especially the human condition. We became sinners by nature, as each of us inherited a sinful spiritual DNA. We were born with it, and our behavior flowed from it.

From there, the dominoes really began to fall. Our sin nature fueled our sinful behavior, and that behavior was willful rebellion against God and his laws. The law of God had been broken, willfully and consistently. This left us guilty before the court of the almighty, destined for the full wrath of God, and deservedly so. It is crucial to understand the law of God shouts condemnation to us all without offering any remedy. His righteous wrath justly hangs over us all, and there is nothing we ourselves can do. We have created a debt we can neither escape nor pay, except by suffering the death of eternal judgment.

Unlike God's law that trumpets the bad news of our guilt and shame, God's gospel is good news. While the reality, that our sin has racked up an eternal penalty torments us, seemingly without remedy, the gospel races in with the only solution possible. That solution comes to us in the biblical word *propitiation*. This word literally means "satisfaction" and speaks to the law's demands being satisfied.

While used only a handful of times in the New Testament, *propitiation* is nevertheless at the heart of the gospel. It declares God not only moved to deal with our sin, but also acted to satisfy the eternal demands of his law. He did this fully and justly through the willingness of Jesus Christ to suffer on the cross.

Imagine if a judge in your town was presiding over the trial of a serial murderer. Now imagine the public reaction if, at the end of the trial, he brought the defendant up to his bench and said *"I am feeling really loving toward you today, and so I am going to set you free despite the preponderance of evidence demonstrating your guilt."* Of course there would be public outrage, and rightly so.

This is often how we understand the gospel. We are quick to offer unbeliever's forgiveness based on Jesus having died for their sins. We suggest this magnanimous gesture on his part is a demonstration of God's great love. God is so loving that he is willing to let you go free if you will only believe in Jesus and commit to follow him. In so packaging the gospel promise, we are forgetting God cannot allow his justice to go unmet. The laws that were broken demand a proper satisfaction. They demand that judgment fall, and the sentences be fully carried out. Both God's love for sinners and his justice must be satisfied.

Paul succinctly expresses both sides of the gospel's good news in 2 Corinthians 5:21: *"For our sake he* — God the Father — *made him* — God the Son — *to be sin who knew no sin, so that in him we might become the righteousness of God."*

What an amazing, incredible transaction! Through the voluntary death of Jesus on the cross, God both punished sin fully, and rescued all those, from every age and nation, who were marked out for salvation from before the foundation of the world. God the Father took our sin and accounted it as belonging to God the Son. Then, on the cross, the full, unobstructed righteous wrath of God the Father fell on God the Son thus satisfying the demands of the law. In that one sacrificial act our sin was brought in its entirety before the court of heaven, recognized as applied to Christ's account, and sentenced appropriately. Our sin was then covered, taken away, and removed from us as far as the east is from the west.

Wait, there is more. At the cross, our sin was not only expiated, that is, wiped off our slate, but also the wrath of God was also fully propitiated, that is satisfied concerning the law's demands. Our sin wiped away and still God's sentence fulfilled. Imagine it! The demands of God's law and God's wrath were fully satisfied so that God's love and grace could be granted to us who were unworthy of either.

The good news of salvation begins with God, moves to our sin and then on to Christ's work by which God's justice and wrath are fully satisfied concerning our sin. That is really only the first half. Too often, our understanding of the gospel ends there, but the New Testament is clear that we had two problems, not one.

Our first problem — our sinful record — was solved through the death of Christ. What about our second fundamental problem our sinful heart? Even given the wrath of God has been satisfied by the death of Christ on our behalf, how will we ever live up to the demands of God's law. How can our sin-drenched nature ever be recognized as living up to the righteousness God demands? The answer is the second great jewel in the crown of salvation.

Just as at the cross our sin was attributed to Christ, so also Christ's righteousness was attributed to us by God Almighty. It might simply be said that saving faith is the radical conviction that God will keep his promise to accept Jesus' death as mine, as well as, accept Jesus' perfect righteousness as mine.

This is Paul's meaning in the verse quoted above, 2 Corinthians 5:21. The first half is God the Son becoming "*sin for us*", the second is that we "*become the righteousness of God*" in him. Paul further glories in this amazing transaction when he exclaims in Philippians 3:9 that he has been "*found in him (Jesus Christ) not having a righteousness of my own that comes from the Law, but that which comes through faith in Christ, the righteousness from God that depends on faith.*" In these two parts, we see the full message of good news. God has solved both problems, tearing away both obstacles to our redemption and reconciliation.

By his death in our place and for our benefit Jesus *propitiated*, or fully satisfied the justice of God, and at the same time enabled the love of God to be poured out on us who could never deserve it on our own. This is the wonder of the cross. This is the grandeur of Christ's substitutionary death. He took our place and took our punishment, and gave us his righteousness. Now when God looks at us he sees us "in Christ." With the righteousness of Christ wrapped around us like a giant blanket we are accepted before a holy God as beloved children. We are accepted, not because of our own worth but wholly because we belong to Christ.

The truths of our sin and Christ's substitutionary death on our behalf are much more than theology, although they are every bit of that. They do form the academic foundation of our standing before God. Yet, if we take the time to revel in them, in their intimate reality and relationship to our very lives, they can become much more than doctrinal convictions. They can form a cycle that keeps us increasingly sensitive to sin, intentionally glorying in Christ, and humbled by the process.

The reality of our sin — it's depth and consequences — should lay hold of us every day, reminding us without Christ we could do nothing to bring a smile to the face of God. Even as those he has rescued, sin continues to play a part in our lives. We know ourselves. We are proud, selfish, and easily tempted to rationalize away our sinful behaviors. We harbor secret sins, making room for them even as we polish the façade of our holiness. We are hypocrites who fail to live up to even our own best standards much less those of our Savior and King.

As we meditate daily on the work of Christ on our behalf we realize he died to free us from bondage to sin. Why? Simply because sin is harmful to us! Sinful thoughts and actions are like a cancer, which starts small but grows to pollute all it touches if not dealt with radically. Understanding the utter sinfulness of sin should humble our pride as we realize we are not all we claim to be. It will also send us running back to the cross, back to the words of Jesus as he cries out "It is finished!"

There, on the cross, God's wrath was satisfied. There on the cross our sentence was fully served. There on the cross our Savior withstood what was rightfully ours. He did it to rescue us from the domain of darkness and the power of sin.

The gospel, as it is driven deeply down into our souls, can actually diminish the Christ-followers desire to sin. Yes, that is right. Our sinful desires stem from the fact we really do not understand how heinous sin really is, or how poisonous it is to us. When we look at the cross, and all Jesus endured for us, our eyes are opened to its toxic nature.

Then, as we recognize the great love of God the Father and God the Son, whereby our rescue was effected and our freedom granted, our hearts are filled with wonder, awe, and love as the magnificence of grace cascades over our hearts and minds. We find ourselves once again content, safe, and loved, in the garden of grace, we call the gospel.

7

■ ■ • • •

CALLED &
CONSPICUOUS

[8]Therefore do not be ashamed of the testimony about our Lord, nor of me his prisoner, but share in suffering for the gospel by the power of God, [9]*who saved us and called us to a holy calling,* not because of our works but because of his own purpose and grace, which he gave us in Christ Jesus before the ages began, [10]and which now has been manifested through the appearing of our Savior Christ Jesus, who abolished death and brought life and immortality to light through the gospel, [11]for which I was appointed a preacher and apostle and teacher, [12]which is why I suffer as I do. But I am not ashamed, for I know whom I have believed, and I am convinced that he is able to guard until that Day what has been entrusted to me.
(2 Timothy 1:8–12)

I grew up in a Baptist pastor's family. That means when the church doors were open, we were there …

Sunday morning, Sunday evening, Sunday school, prayer meeting, youth group, potlucks, week-long evangelistic meetings, work days, choir practice, and any number of other special services. When I used to read David's word in the Psalms about *"dwelling in the house of the Lord,"* I was sure it was written about our family.

Along the way, I also heard the gospel many times, and I grew up thoroughly versed in what "salvation" meant. At least I thought I did. If you were to ask me, I would have told you that we were "saved from sin and hell." That was how I defined being saved. We used to say Jesus was "fire insurance" against the fires of hell.

I grew up convinced salvation was "from" something bad, but somehow I missed the fact that God saves his people "for" something amazingly good. He saves us for the purpose of demonstrating what holiness looks like in everyday living. Paul put it very simply. God has saved us *and called us to a holy calling!*

At this point in Paul's discussion of the gospel, he moves from *propitiation* to *pardon.* We who were formerly enemies are now friends. We once were guilty, but now are justified. Previously we were strangers and aliens, without hope in this world, and under the wrath of God. Now in Christ, we have been brought near, cleansed, pardoned, and amazingly, adopted into the very family of the Judge himself, the God of all creation. This inclusion in a new family comes with the prospect of a new set of family characteristics, and it is to this that Paul now speaks.

Paul moves easily from salvation by God to vibrant, righteous living for God. Apparently, Paul is unaware that some believe salvation can be owned without there being any substantial change in behavior. He gives no place to the idea that our justification can be separated from our sanctification, that our freedom from sin can be separated from our freedom to obey Christ. He simply declares that those who are rescued by God have also been called to live a godly life. What can this mean but that the purpose of our salvation is that we may share his holiness?

Sanctification is the work of God the Spirit through the Word by which the Christ-follower becomes increasingly "for" God and as a result, averse to sin.

To be holy is not measured first by our separation from sinful desires and behavior. Rather, it is measured by our increasing love for God, and delight in obedience to all he offers us. When we try to run away from sin, we almost always fail unless we are replacing the desire for sin with a greater desire for righteousness. Faith — true saving faith — is a life-dominating conviction that all

God has for us through holy obedience to him is so much better than anything sin can guarantee. To be holy is to see, in a deepening relationship with God, a better way to live than dwelling in the toxicity of selfishness and sin.

What does this *holy calling* consist of? It starts with Paul's understanding that our salvation has brought us into the very family of God through adoption. In Ephesians 1:5 he declares that *"He predestined us for adoption as sons through Jesus Christ according to the purpose of His will …"* From the beginning God planned that those he elected in love, and redeemed through the Son's substitutionary death, would not only be pardoned in the forensic sense, but adopted in the familial sense. As judge, God declared us righteous. As Father, he has brought us into his family.

The doctrine of *adoption* describes the fact that, given new life in Christ, believers now have an entirely new identity. They are no longer rebels, but beloved sons and daughters. Not only has the wrath of God been satisfied and their crimes pardoned, they have been adopted into the family of the King. This grants them the full inheritance of glory to be sure. This also calls them to live out the family traits, the first being holiness. God saves sinners, makes them his own sons and daughters, and expects them to live conspicuous lives, displaying the character of Jesus Christ himself, beginning with a passion for God best described as holiness.

Peter declares this truth in 1 Peter 1:14–17:

> [14]"As obedient children, do not be conformed to the passions of your former ignorance, [15]but as he who called you is holy, you also be holy in all your conduct, [16]since it is written, "You shall be holy, for I am holy." [17]And if you call on him as Father who judges impartially according to each one's deeds, conduct yourselves with fear throughout the time of your exile ..."

The Father who has called us and adopted us into his family has called us to exhibit the family characteristics. Our ability to bear the image of God has been enhanced by the new life we have been given in Christ, and it grants us the privilege of walking as children of God in holiness.

In Paul's day, adoption was much different than it is today. Instead of couples adopting young children, the Roman society saw adoption as a way for the strong and wealthy to carry on their lineage. Those in the Roman world who had no heir would adopt a young man who showed great promise for the express purpose of leaving to him the family name and estate. Adoption was for the purpose of inheritance and came with the legal standing necessary to be a true heir.

Paul understood this sense of adoption and considered the believer's adoption into the family of God to be paramount in the salvation transaction. God chose us, redeemed us, reformed us, and pardoned us *so that* he could adopt us into his family, to carry his name and extend his estate. He adopted us to be joint-heirs with Jesus Christ himself.

The call to holiness is simply the call to demonstrate the validity of your adoption into the family of God. Is God your father? Then it will be seen in your behavior. Do you love God your father? Then it will be demonstrated in the delight you find in pursuing his will, and imitating his ways. Are you at home in the family of God, with the brothers and sisters whom he has likewise adopted? Then you will love the church, and see your life as all about making her the spotless bride she should be. Is your father the King? Then you will be diligent in advancing his mission and kingdom through the gospel.

The idea of our having been adopted into the family of God turns the focus of salvation from us to God. Adoptees usually do not get to choose whether they will go to the adoptive family. They are just overwhelmed that someone would love them and elevate them to the position of heir. Those adopted understand that, while their situation has been bettered by far, all the focus should be on the loving father who planned, and carried out the adoptive plan.

Despite some popular presentations of the gospel, it is not true that God saved us for us. His purposes in salvation were much greater. He saved us for his own glory, for his own name's sake.

In Ephesians 2:1–6 we read we were all dead in our sins, unwilling and unable to remedy our situation, and headed for the just wrath of God. God stepped into our world and personal histories in the person of Jesus Christ who has rescued us solely as a result of his grace. In verse 7 — a verse almost universally passed over in our desire to land on the familiar verses 8-10 — Paul ventures an answer to the question that often goes unasked: *Just why did God do all this for us, unworthy as we are?* The answer is so clear: *"so that in the coming ages He might show the immeasurable riches of His grace in kindness toward us in Christ Jesus."* God saved us, in the way he saved us, in order to show off the surpassing riches of his grace throughout eternity.

This idea that God wants to show off the greatness and glory of his grace is the foundation of Paul's statement in Ephesians 2:10 that we are "his workmanship." As those who have been rescued and adopted into the family of God, we are God's showpieces, samples of what he, and he alone, can do in rescuing and reforming sin-drenched people into finished examples of what his sovereign power and matchless love can accomplish.

It must be said, God did not save us so we could feel good. He saved us so he could look good. Someone has stated it well: *We have been saved from the wrath of God, by the grace of God, for the glory of God.* Paul absolutely connects our salvation to our maturity in holiness. God saves us for the purpose of making us holy. Wait, there's more.

No, God did not save us so that we could feel good. Yes, he saved us so that he could look good. It is also true that when he looks good in us, we will feel the best in him. Again, John Piper said it best: *"We will be most satisfied when God is most glorified."*

So, here is the rejuvenating part. Ever feel fatigued in your battle to stay unstained by the culture of our world? Ever become spiritually tired and thereby susceptible to the temptations of the flesh? Ever feel like the odds are so stacked against you that success seems out of the question? Remember this: the God of your salvation is the God of your sanctification. He has saved you for himself, to be his chosen bride, to be his workmanship. He has granted you all the provision you need to run that race, fight the fight, and be conspicuous for him. When times seem overwhelming, and your heart grows faint, journey on to the rock of your salvation. Get there, stay there, and find rest.

Paul, in Philippians 2:14–16, gives this same distinctive pep talk:

> [14]"Do all things without grumbling or disputing, [15]that you may be blameless and innocent, children of God without blemish in the midst of a crooked and twisted generation, among whom you shine as lights in the world, [16] holding fast to the word of life, so that in the day of Christ I may be proud that I did not run in vain or labor in vain."

Be careful here. First, understand all the provision you need is found in Christ, not in yourself. Apart from him, we cannot do anything. Found in him, we can walk worthy of our holy calling knowing that it is God who is at work in us both to will and to work for his good pleasure.

How can we know God's sanctifying power is at work in our lives? It is simple really. We will know the Spirit is working mightily in our lives when we are laboring and striving to run the race in holiness and truth. That was Paul's point in Colossians 1:29:

> "For this I toil, struggling with all his energy that he powerfully works within me."

We can be assured the Spirit is working his sanctifying ways in us when we are passionately and consistently determined to love, honor, and obey the Lord Jesus from the heart. In every circumstance, we can know the God who has saved us will complete his reforming work in us. He who began the work will absolutely see it through to completion, for he has saved us and called us with a holy calling.

Second, while the effects of the gospel will diminish our desire for sin, we will never become sinless this side of heaven. We are called to live the redeemed life through as yet unredeemed flesh, and that will often result in failure to meet God's holy standards. As we are more and more shaped by the truths of the gospel, and more and more conformed to the image of Jesus, our consciences will be more and more soft toward holiness, and hardened against sin. While perfection cannot be obtained, progress must be accomplished, for our own good and for the glory of God.

Our God has saved us intentionally, and he has adopted us into his family. He has granted us an eternal inheritance, and calls us to live holy lives as we carry the banner of his family and kingdom. What an amazing truth. What a singular privilege. What a wonderful gospel. What a magnificent God!

8

— — — • •

IF IT'S TO BE
IT'S UP TO GOD

[8]Therefore do not be ashamed of the testimony about our Lord, nor of me his prisoner, but share in suffering for the gospel by the power of God, [9]who saved us and called us to a holy calling, not *because of our works* but because of his own purpose and grace, which he gave us in Christ Jesus before the ages began, [10]and which now has been manifested through the appearing of our Savior Christ Jesus, who abolished death and brought life and immortality to light through the gospel, [11]for which I was appointed a preacher and apostle and teacher, [12]which is why I suffer as I do. But I am not ashamed, for I know whom I have believed, and I am convinced that he is able to guard until that Day what has been entrusted to me.
(2 Timothy 1:8–12)

I admit it. I thrive on recognition. For some, just being on the team is enough. For others, the team has to win in order for them to feel satisfied. Still others of us thirst to be recognized for winning. Let's be honest, at some level we all seek recognition. We want others to look at us and say, "Way to go; you were great!"

This pride of accomplishment runs deep in the human heart and lies behind our desire to take credit wherever we can. Sometimes we try to take credit for things we had no hand in. My friend Sean calls this "the rooster taking credit for the dawn." There is a lot of that happening in our world, especially as politicians and pundits spin the daily news in their favor.

There is one thing no human can ever take credit for: *Salvation in Christ Jesus.*

Timothy was an overwhelmed, timid, quasi-ashamed minister of the gospel in Ephesus. His fire was almost out, and his mentor Paul wrote him a letter of rejuvenation. Unlike what we might expect, Paul did not come alongside Timothy with a compassionate call to rest or to take a cruise or go on a sabbatical. He first demands he quit being ashamed and timid and then directs his heart and mind back to the gospel.

God is the One who has drafted him, and equipped him for every good work (see: 3:16,17). God is the One who rescued him, and called him to a life of holiness. God has done all this, and none of it has been conditioned on Timothy's worth, conduct, or expertise. None of it happened *because of his works.* Timothy may be able to take credit for some things in his life and ministry, but his position in Christ is not one of them.

Today I often hear Christ-followers try to shoehorn their works into the redemptive plan of God. *"Sure God chose to save me because He knew me before I even was, and knew that I would respond to the gospel."* While this is popular, it really has no biblical support. Scripture is clear: We love God because he first loved us. His sovereign action, through the Spirit and the gospel, enabled our repentance and faith. It had to be this way or no one could ever experience redemption. Dead in sins, both unable and unwilling to obey God from the heart, our rescue was completely dependent on God making the first move.

Like Lazarus in the grave, we first needed the grace of regeneration in order to hear the voice of Christ and respond in faith. Far from being something to rail against, this understanding of God's sovereign love is where humility and awe begin. We belong to him solely because of his undeserved grace. Salvation is of the Lord.

Just as distressing, I hear believers argue their works of righteousness are what keep God happy and account for the blessings they are enjoying. This is the very thing Paul is arguing against!

It is curious that Paul would be telling Pastor Timothy that our works do not factor into God's treatment of us unless he knew Timothy was starting to feel resentful toward God. Perhaps Timothy was mad God was not rewarding him more for his deeds. Maybe he had fallen into the trap of legalism and felt God was into the "quid pro quo" way of handing out rewards. You know, the "if I do this, God has to do that" way of thinking.

Perhaps you have fallen into this trap. Perhaps you think if you read your Bible every day then God owes you good things. If you pray daily, sign up for a mission trip, and give a bit more money than usual to the church then

God's goodies will become more prevalent in your life. If so, then you and Timothy both need to be reminded that our standing in Christ is sufficient, and already complete.

God's favor to us can never be more than it already is in Christ. Paul told the Ephesians God had already blessed them *"in Christ with every spiritual blessing"* (Ephesians 1:3) and also given them *"everything to enjoy"* (1 Timothy 6:17). Here is the truth: On our very best day, when we believe we have gone above and beyond in our obedience and spiritual fervor, he still accepts us because of Christ and his righteousness. The better news is this: on our very worst day, when temptation has had its way with us, we are still just as accepted by God because of Christ and His righteousness. This is really good news!

So, why do some reject the idea our acceptance and security before God are based solely on the work of Christ and the fact his righteousness has been accounted as ours?

First, it makes it appear sinful living has no consequence and believers can sin with impunity. This is only an appearance and not reality.

If we look through the lens of Scripture here is what we find. Those who are truly regenerate have the Spirit dwelling in them. The Spirit realigns our affections away from sin and toward righteousness. This means true Christ-followers will never be satisfied with sin. We may dabble in it. We may even walk in it. We can never live in it.

If we do dabble in it and allow it to find a home in our lives, we had better look out for our father. Our God is a great father. Like every good father, God will not allow his children to stray far and tarnish the family name. He will discipline us so we may once again be examples of holiness (see: Hebrews 12:4–11).

Second, people hate the idea of God's unmerited favor simply because they crave recognition. They desperately want their righteousness to get some credit. I can certainly understand this point. I have already admitted there is in me a natural drive to be recognized. While this is something I have to mortify daily, it also makes me appreciate what God is really doing in the gospel. By accomplishing everything graciously, he puts me and every believer in a position of radical dependence upon Christ.

This is exactly what Paul wanted Timothy to understand. Timothy was fatigued and ashamed and seemingly backing away from the tasks and challenges of gospel ministry. He needed rest, but the right kind of rest. He needed to once again rest in the finished and consistently applied work of Jesus Christ on behalf of all who would ever believe.

He needed to recognize that, while his obedience and diligence were required, they were never the variables that mattered most in the success of the gospel. He needed to rely on the power of God and the unalterable righteousness of Christ.

So, I know what you are thinking: *Doesn't our righteous living and diligent obedience matter? Doesn't holy living bring about God's smile?* Of course, the answer to both questions is a resounding "Yes, it does!" Our heavenly Father has called us to holiness, to a passionate seeking after him. It pleases him, and he requires it of us. He also insists we labor diligently as his workmanship, his samples, to bring the grace and love of Christ to our world.

There is no place for couch potato Christianity. We are to run the race before us, fight the good fight, and persevere to the end. Like Paul, we are to strive mightily to accomplish the work we have been given to do (see: Philippians 2:12–13; Colossians 1:29; Hebrews 12:1–3). We are never to think our work is what grants us God's favor. Rather, our work is our response of love and respect to the God who has saved us and called us to holiness quite apart from any of our own works, either good or bad.

Where are you? Has misunderstanding the basis of your acceptance before God put you on the performance treadmill? Are you running the race hoping to keep God on your side?

If so, you are most likely either spiritually exhausted, or already greatly disillusioned and cynical with the whole set of evangelical rules. Chances are good you are also a bit confused given you have been pretty lazy lately, and God hasn't seemed to notice.

What to do with the situation at hand? The answer is simple: Come back into the garden of grace called the gospel. Look into your heart and see if you are truly trusting in the righteousness of Christ to fully satisfy God. Are you certain Jesus Christ has paid your sinful record in full? Do you trust the promise of God that he has accepted both Christ's death and righteousness as though they were yours and adopted you into his family as a true son or daughter?

If the answers are yes, then rest in his arms. Understand his unconditional love and forgiveness.

Recognize you have been born again to a living hope that is imperishable and reserved in heaven for you. Grasp this astounding truth: *you will never be more forgiven or accepted than you already are.*

Then feel the response of love growing in your heart as you recognize obeying Christ and pursuing his mission in your life is really a grand privilege as well as your very best and most satisfying option. Find the truest help possible in the rejuvenation power of the gospel.

9

— — — — •

SAVED ON
PURPOSE

[8]Therefore do not be ashamed of the testimony about our Lord, nor of me his prisoner, but share in suffering for the gospel by the power of God, [9]who saved us and called us to a holy calling, not because of our *works but because of his own purpose and grace,* which he gave us in Christ Jesus before the ages began, [10]and which now has been manifested through the appearing of our Savior Christ Jesus, who abolished death and brought life and immortality to light through the gospel, [11]for which I was appointed a preacher and apostle and teacher, [12]which is why I suffer as I do. But I am not ashamed, for I know whom I have believed, and I am convinced that he is able to guard until that Day what has been entrusted to me.

(2 Timothy 1:8–12)

Not long ago some friends were dining with Cherylyn and me at a nice restaurant. We had not seen them in many years, and as their travels brought them our way, we were able to share a meal and many great memories. As our time ended, I asked our server for the bill. Her face lit up with a mischievous smile, *"Your bill was already paid by a couple sitting across the restaurant. They said to tell you "Grace to you.""*

Among our church family *"grace to you"* is a common greeting, and is used to close all our services. It is a family thing, a way for the family of Grace Baptist Church to advertise our relationship with, and love for, one another.

In this case, they had demonstrated the truest meaning of our "grace" greeting, and there was nothing I could do differently. In fact, to this day I am not sure who paid the bill because they chose to remain anonymous.

Our generous benefactors had made up their minds to gift us our meal. They did it on purpose, and I expect they felt great joy in so doing. We also felt something. First we were surprised, then shocked, and finally we felt undeserving. That is what grace is supposed to do. It is supposed to be shocking, and leave us feeling as though we have gotten what we never could have deserved.

In this verse, Paul reminds Timothy of the marvelous, shocking, and downright undeserved grace of God that fuels every bit of our new life in Christ. We might wonder just why Paul thought it necessary to remind Pastor Timothy of this fundamental component of salvation. Did he not already know, and teach this? Of course he did! Somewhere along the line though, he had stopped being rejuvenated by the daily comprehension of God's amazing grace.

For Paul, the gospel is not just the story of God's grace

to the unbeliever. It is also a daily means of refreshment to the believing heart. In the gospel, we are reminded of God's greatness, our brokenness, and the privilege we have been afforded to live out a redeemed life. Timothy was in great need of these reminders. He was burned out. He needed to be directed away from his own efforts and plans and back into the garden of God's grace in the gospel.

Paul has stated it very simply. God is the one who has saved Timothy, and in so doing called him to holy living. He has been rescued and is now being reformed according to the image of Jesus Christ. God is doing great things in Timothy, and Paul reminds him he cannot take credit for any of it. His standing in the family of God was not earned and cannot be improved; it was fully accomplished forever by Jesus Christ.

Now Paul goes on to give another piece of the story. Far from salvation being earned, bought, or merited through our best efforts, it is in its entirety conditioned only on God's sovereign purpose and made active through his grace.

Let us look at some words in order to get the whole picture. Notice the "not ... but" construction in vs. 9. Paul is clear. "Not this ... but this." Not our works, but God's purpose. Paul is setting out a stark contrast between what we do and what God does in accomplishing the work of our being justified and set apart unto God.

Next, let's look at the words "purpose and grace." In several places Paul states God has a definite, intentional plan for history. In Ephesians 1:5 it is called the *"purpose of his will."* In the same chapter, he states God works *"all things according to the counsel of his will"* (vs. 11). Later in Ephesians 3:11, Paul refers to this plan as the *"eternal purpose that he has realized in Christ Jesus our Lord."*

Further, we find this "purpose plan" was fully formed and implemented before time began. Paul describes this in the text we are studying: (2 Timothy 1:9), as *"before the ages began,"* as well as in many other places (see: John 17:24; Ephesians 1:4; 1 Peter 1:20).

All this adds up to one undeniable truth: God has been operating in history according to a specific, sovereign plan that was decided upon and enacted even before time began. Before the ages of any history, God was at work accomplishing his purpose through a plan designed to finish something that was worthy of God's attention.

Paul loves the word "grace." Today this is too easily misunderstood. Just what is "grace?" We might be tempted to think of grace as a commodity, something you might gather, or collect. We often speak and sing as though grace was some sort of magical, heavenly dust that God allows to float over us, bringing us power and blessing. It appears many today have this concept of grace, and it drives their way of life. They believe grace can be gained through obedience, and thus find themselves on a performance treadmill, always running after something their preacher has impressed upon them as necessary. They apparently think God pays on commission.

Grace is not a substance. Grace cannot be purchased by the pound no matter how obedient we are. Grace is actually the activity of God's benevolence, the extension of his loving attitude toward his children. It is the way

God acts when his face is "toward" us rather than turned "away" from us. Grace is the loving and merciful action of God toward those who do not deserve it, cannot earn it, and can never muster it up themselves or somehow prepare themselves to receive grace.

The word "grace" helps us understand the center of God's plan. We might ask, *"Just what was worth God's intentionality in putting in place such a massive plan?"* The answer can only be that God's glory is best seen in the salvation of those who neither deserve rescue nor can accomplish it themselves. Our holy God has determined he wants to be known for accepting the unholy and reforming them to share his holiness. Further, he wants to be known for accomplishing this quite apart from any merit, work, or worth on their part. This is what grace means. He wants to do it freely and graciously, unconditioned upon anything other than his own will to do so. His purpose demands his grace does it all.

The consequences of rightly understanding grace are momentous. Recognizing grace as God's activity toward us in Christ rescues us from the selfish lie that somehow our behavior can move us to where God's grace is no longer our primary boast. The flipside of this error is thinking our obedience gains us more packets of grace in terms of God's temporal blessing on our lives. Neither of these is true. The good news is simply that the grace of God — his benevolent, merciful, loving, redeeming, providing, protecting activity — is immutable toward those who are in Christ and in whom the Spirit dwells.

Remember, on your very best day, when you have

lived up to God's standards as best you can in all things, your standing before God is still based solely on the merits of Christ. However, as mentioned previously, what is even better is that on your worst day, when you have failed miserably to honor God, your standing before God is still based solely on the merits of Christ. Such is the nature of grace, and such is the core of the gospel. We can never meditate on this too much.

So, how do you think these words of the Apostle fell on the heart of Pastor Timothy? How do they fall on your heart? Does it make your pride sit up and start boasting that you have actually been a good "save" for God? That he is pretty fortunate to have found you and adopted you into the family? Or, is it quite humbling to recognize clearly that God could have left you in the stream of sin, willfully floating on the current of self-centeredness, foolishly refusing to believe you were heading for that steep, thundering waterfall called eternal judgment? Do just a few chills cause you to shudder when you understand just how long it has been since your sense of self importance was flattened by the grandeur of God's undeserved power in your life?

The idea our standing before God is a result, not of our works, but of God's sovereign purpose is a truth that often does not sit well in our day. We ultra-moderns, in the West especially, are raised on the bread of equality where everyone deserves the same chance as everyone else. We believe we all enter life on good footing, in a land where dreams come true, and, further, that society owes it to us all to provide whatever is necessary for our success.

Awash in this egalitarianism, it is often hard to

understand the reality that God is not a president ... he's a king! Many of our brothers and sisters living in restrictive cultures understand this very well. They have long ago jettisoned any sense that the Kingdom of God is actually being duplicated in the platform of any political party or human administration. They do not look to human government as a vehicle of grace and salvation. They have been freed from that and joyfully recognize their standing as strangers and aliens in this world and dedicated servants of King Jesus.

Regardless of where you live, it is true we all enter life on equal footing. Yet, that footing is nothing on which we are to boast. We all come to this life as sinners whose trajectory is heading toward God's wrath unless our nature is radically changed. The direction of our lives has already been set by the corruption that comes pre-installed on our human hard drive. The virus of sin has already infected our operating system, and left to ourselves we willingly and joyfully pursue our own course, pull our own strings, and try to find all the pleasure we can in this life ... all with fists raised in rebellion to our loving Creator.

We will never come to understand our true nature unless the light of grace dawns in our hearts. Apart from this, we believe we are good and valuable and have rights. Given this, it is understandable why so many believe God owes them something. He owes them a good life in exchange for some religious acts and mostly moral actions. This is the god of Moralistic Therapeutic Deism, and he certainly is not allowed to have a plan that does not include human happiness and success. After all, this is the ultra-modern era, and we all deserve the same opportunities.

In the end, we too often act as though God works for us and is obligated to us even though largely forgotten by us. In reality, this just is not true.

When a society begins to humanize God in order to deify man, it ends up minimizing sin. When we erode God's sovereignty in order to promote our rights, all we end up with is a man-centered story that makes God our servant, his church our club, and our well-being his goal.

Maybe Timothy was falling into this. Maybe the Ephesian culture was pulling him into its mold. We do not know. What we do know is Paul thought it was important to remind him of the gospel story in all of its simplicity and beauty.

God has a plan, and it will be worked out perfectly. Our acceptance before him was planned long before time, and it is the enormity of that very thought that either infuriates or humbles us. If it humbles us, we are all the better for it. If we are made small against the backdrop of Almighty God's sovereign, eternal plan, then we are all the more able to be refreshed by knowing this omnipotent, wholly other God is to us a personal, loving, providing, and protecting father.

Our privilege as Christ-followers is to live every day humbled that we have been included in his family, adoring him and courageously extending his gracious offer of life to those around us. Moreover, just in case you have forgotten, we are called to do it with smiles on our faces testifying to the unquenchable joy that comes from living in the garden of grace we call the gospel.

10

IT'S ALL IN CHRIST JESUS

[8]Therefore do not be ashamed of the testimony about our Lord, nor of me his prisoner, but share in suffering for the gospel by the power of God, [9]who saved us and called us to a holy calling, not because of our works but because of his own purpose and grace, *which he gave us in Christ Jesus* before the ages began, [10]and which now has been manifested through the appearing of our Savior Christ Jesus, who abolished death and brought life and immortality to light through the gospel, [11]for which I was appointed a preacher and apostle and teacher, [12]which is why I suffer as I do. But I am not ashamed, for I know whom I have believed, and I am convinced that he is able to guard until that Day what has been entrusted to me.
(2 Timothy 1:8–12)

Two years ago, a friend gave me a very generous gift. It was not my birthday, and there was really no reason behind it other than he wanted to show how much he appreciated me. It was so exciting to open, and yet it was hard to take.

I immediately began to think of what I could have done to deserve such a gift. I actually felt bad I was the object of such a lavish expression of love, and immediately started thinking about how I could be extravagant back to him and make it all even.

Isn't that just like us? We feel we have to earn our gifts, or at least do something that makes us feel like we "deserve" the extravagance. The problem is our pride. To have something wonderful given to us while completely undeserving and unable to reciprocate rubs us the wrong way. We live in a quid pro quo world, and when things are too one-sided, we actually feel bad.

This explains why Paul had to remind Timothy that every ounce of his acceptance before Almighty God was made possible by a love grant from heaven. His rescue from the ravages of sin as well as his position in the family of a holy God had been completely accomplished by God. His good works played no part. Instead, he had been graciously gifted a new, eternally satisfying life in Christ Jesus quite apart from any merit of his own.

Perhaps Timothy had forgotten this wonderful part of the gospel story. Perhaps as he went about his ministerial duties in Ephesus he began to consider God certainly had made a good choice when he decided to draft him into service. Whatever the case, it is clear Paul thought he needed to hear the simple truth that all he had received from God had been granted to him. He did not deserve it, and he certainly could not reciprocate in kind.

The whole idea God is indebted to us has gained a wide, if uninformed, acceptance. I would suggest the vast majority of evangelical Christ-followers actually believe God saved them in response to their decision to let him. They were wandering through life, mostly doing okay. At some point, things took a turn for the worse. They decided to give religion a go, and maybe read something, talked to a friend, or in some fashion got them onto a path that took them to the story of Jesus. They listened, analyzed, considered, reflected, and eventually decided to try it. They decided to give Jesus a chance to live up to his billing. They made the decision to put Jesus into the game of their life to see if he could get the win. If that story sounds good to you, watch out. Better yet, go back and read 2 Timothy 1:9.

I do not know what was going through Timothy's mind, but two things are clear: First, although he had been appointed by God, he was now ashamed of the gospel, back on his heels, and basically burned out.

Second, he was in desperate need of clarity when it came to the gospel. His position in grace, like yours and mine, was never conditioned on our works. It was never even conditioned upon our belief, since our faith itself was included in God's gift (see: Ephesians 2:8–10, and further explanation below).

Rather than our salvation being a result of our works, the entirety of our rescue — including our faith and repentance — was the result of God's work, accomplished by God the Son and applied through the gospel by God the Spirit. Paul might easily have stated it this way:

"God the Father thought it, God the Son bought it, God the Spirit brought it ... and Timothy my son ... you've got it. Now, enjoy it, live up to it, rest in it, and stop trying to earn it. You have been gifted what you could never earn nor buy. Now, let that wash over you as you rest in the garden of grace we call the gospel."

Maybe you are confused about something I said regarding faith and repentance above. Let me try to clear it up by first listening to Paul, and then making some explanatory comments:

[2]And you were dead in the trespasses and sins [2]in which you once walked, following the course of this world, following the prince of the power of the air, the spirit that is now at work in the sons of disobedience — [3]among whom we all once lived in the passions of our flesh, carrying out the desires of the body and the mind, and were by nature children of wrath, like the rest of mankind. [4]But God, being rich in mercy, because of the great love with which he loved us, [5]even when we were dead in our trespasses, made us alive together with Christ — by grace you have been saved — [6]and raised us up with him and seated us with him in the heavenly places in Christ Jesus, [7]so that in the coming ages he might show the immeasurable riches of his grace in kindness toward us in Christ Jesus. [8]For by grace you have been saved through faith. And this is not your own doing; it is the gift of God, [9]not a result of works, so that no one may boast. [10]For we are his workmanship, created in Christ Jesus for good works, which God prepared beforehand, that we should walk in them.

(Ephesians 2:1–10)

[24]And the Lord's servant must not be quarrelsome but kind to everyone, able to teach, patiently enduring evil, [25]correcting his opponents with gentleness. God may perhaps grant them repentance leading to a knowledge of the truth, [26]and they may come to their senses and escape from the snare of the devil, after being captured by him to do his will.
(2 Timothy 2.24–26)

The truth is, being dead in our sins (Ephesians 2:1–3) we could never have worked up repentance over our sin, or saving faith in Jesus Christ on our own. It is clear from Paul's instructions above that both saving faith and true repentance are gifts given by God. As you can see, faith is a gift of God, and repentance has been granted by God. Both faith and repentance are the work of God the Spirit as he comes riding in on the gospel to do a regenerating work in a human heart:

[8]For by grace you have been saved through faith. *And this is not your own doing; it is the gift of God,* [9]not a result of works, so that no one may boast.
(Ephesians 2:8–9)

God may perhaps grant them repentance leading to a knowledge of the truth,
(2 Timothy 2:25b)

However, it is not true this makes faith and repentance unnecessary or even something other than our own actions.

Since our repentance and our faith start with our own mental decisions, they are, in every sense, ours. They arc the product of our will. As we grow in the knowledge of God and his great rescue mission, we come to see he enabled our sin-corrupted will to want righteousness. We came to love him because he first loved us.

We came to know him because he first knew us. We came to see the reality of our sin and the magnificence of our Savior because he first gave us new life, opening our blind spiritual eyes and ears to see Christ and hear his voice calling us to himself, as Jesus himself said:

> "Truly, truly, I say to you, an hour is coming, and is now here, when the dead will hear the voice of the Son of God, and those who hear will live."
> (John 5:25)

We see this clearly illustrated in the event of Lazarus' rising from the grave in John 11. You remember the story? Mary and Martha had sent word to Jesus that their brother Lazarus was sick. Strangely, when Jesus heard the news he purposely delayed his coming for a few days. By the time he came to Bethany, Lazarus had already been in the tomb four days. That was no barrier to God the Son. He had come to demonstrate the power necessary to reverse the curse of sin and death. As he stood at the entrance of the tomb, he created life with his word, just as at the beginning of creation. He spoke and Lazarus came out of the grave alive.

We need to think about this for a moment. Lazarus was dead, and had been for days. None of his bodily systems were operative, including his ears. How, then, did he hear the voice of Jesus? How did the dead one hear? The only answer is, through his word, Jesus brought life to his body and enabled him to hear *"the voice of the Son of God"* as predicted back in John 5:25. The work of God made possible and actual the active response on the part of Lazarus.

Here is the essence of it all, the *sine qua non:* While they cannot be separated chronologically, logically regeneration must precede faith. God's work preceded our response. His life made our love both possible and actual. His power in giving us life made his offer of redeeming love irresistible. All this was according to the plan granted us in Christ Jesus before the age began.

Notice again Paul was careful to add the *"in Christ Jesus"* part to his magnificent pronouncement of saving grace. That is what keeps us from gloating about our acceptance before God. Something we are all prone to do.

When my son was in high school, his club soccer team travelled to Florida where they ended up winning the National Championship of club soccer. It was a huge deal at the time, and being the proud and fanatical soccer dad, I took every opportunity to let people know that "we" had won it all!

Of course, I had nothing to do with the actual "win." I had not won anything. As excited as I was for my son and his teammates, in reality I could not take any credit for any part of their tremendous accomplishment. Yet, I boasted, gloated, and generally made a nuisance of myself letting everyone know about the great championship victory.

There is a connection between this soccer story and the way we often view our salvation. Our pride maneuvers us into boasting, although we are pretty good at dressing it up in different clothes. We look at others who have no time for the gospel, whose lives are leaking or worse, and it is easy for us to look down on them. It is easy to breathe a sigh of relief over the fact we responded so differently and now have all the advantages of God's salvation. We had the sobriety of mind to hear the message, analyze it carefully, and come to the right conclusion after all. We knew a good deal when we saw it, and we are sure glad we were able to give our lives to Jesus. The reality is, just like my son's championship, we really had nothing to do with accomplishing our rescue. It was given to us, in Christ Jesus.

Paul reminds Timothy, and us, that all we have is "in Christ." Apart from him, we are nothing, have nothing, and can accomplish nothing. Our worth? In Christ. Our joy? In Christ. Our hope? In Christ. Our assurance? In Christ. Our every spiritual blessing? In Christ.

Sinclair Ferguson sums it up beautifully:

"It is in Christ we receive all the blessings of the Christian life. We are chosen in him. In him, we are predestined to be like him. In Christ we are called, and in him born again to newness of life (1 Pet. 1:3). In him, we have faith, and receive the Holy Spirit. In him, we are brought into the privileges of brotherhood in the family of God. In Christ is our sanctification (1 Cor. 1:30). When we see him, we will be made like him, for when he appears in glory, we shall also appear with Christ (1 John 3:2; Col. 3:4). From beginning to end all blessings are ours in Christ." (The Christian Life, pg. 23)

The doctrine of God's sovereignty in salvation is often looked upon with disdain because it seems to minimize our freedom, our choices, and our actions. This stems from a very important issue at the very core of our theology itself. Evangelical theology falls into two broad camps and where you find yourself will depend on whom you are attempting to defend.

If you are prone to defend the nobility of humanity, and the free will of man, you will end up arguing for a type of divine sovereignty that is limited somehow by the free, undetermined actions of mankind. If, on the other hand, your desire is to defend God as the Bible describes him, you will have to figure out how to correlate God's absolute sovereignty over all things with the constant command for sinners to turn from their sin, repent, and place their faith in Christ alone.

It is obvious on which side of the fence I reside. And frankly, the challenge of finding a biblical answer to the relationship between God's sovereignty and man's freedom is much easier than attempting to explain the universe we live in apart from the total sovereignty of God. If there is even one molecule that is outside the superintendency of God's eternal purpose, we are all in huge trouble. If events, decisions, and tragedies are somehow out of God's control, then there is really no reason to entrust him with our lives, either now or for eternity.

Rest assured, we can trust him, especially in this area of the salvation of our souls. Paul had no trouble asserting God's sovereignty in salvation without stopping to defend it. In fact, the statements he is making to Timothy in the text we are studying are meant to encourage the young man. Paul is seeking to lift Timothy up, put a smile on his face, and embolden him to walk courageously into each day.

So, why is it so refreshing, and potentially rejuvenating to know all we have has been granted to us by God, in Jesus Christ? Because it means we can rest. We can rest in the security of God's love. We can rest in the comfort of his finished work on our behalf. We can flop down and find comfort in the soft and accepting grace of God that is as sure and lasting as the promise of God, and the intercession of Christ on our behalf.

Are you discouraged? Has life hit you broadside? Are you running out of fuel to face tomorrow? Tragically, many in your situation find themselves blaming God, turning a cold shoulder to him, and even running away from him. For those who truly understand the gospel, the trials of life become the reason to run to Jesus and find refuge in his unchanging love, sympathetic heart, and promised power.

Again, Sinclair Ferguson reminds us of the practical benefits of being "in Christ" and having all things in him:

> "This should lead us to a deeper humility. Humility is not simply feeling small and useless — like an inferiority complex. It is sensing how great and glorious God is, and seeing myself in that light. Humility in Scripture is the fruit of grace, not of fear. It is God's love, which makes a man truly humble. Now, Scripture emphasizes these aspects of the Christian life to show us the depth and length, the breadth and height of the love of God. When we see that we are humbled by the knowledge that God cares so much about us."

"This should lead us to a steadfast assurance. Lack of assurance is often caused, like a sense of inferiority, by being too taken up with ourselves. But our assurance does not lie in what we are, be we great or small. It lies in what God has done in his plan of salvation to secure us to himself." (The Christian Life, pg. 23)

Timothy needed to hear all this. You and I need to hear it, and we need to reflect on it and find rest in it everyday. Otherwise, our natural tendency to bristle in the face of undeserved generosity may pull us back into the riptide of thinking that we did, or are doing something to keep God on our side. In Christ, he is always on our side, and — as we will see in the next chapter — he has been there "from all eternity."

11

LOVE BEFORE TIME

[8]Therefore do not be ashamed of the testimony about our Lord, nor of me his prisoner, but share in suffering for the gospel by the power of God, [9]who saved us and called us to a holy calling, not because of our works but because of his own purpose and grace, which he gave us in Christ Jesus before *the ages began,* [10]and which now has been manifested through the appearing of our Savior Christ Jesus, who abolished death and brought life and immortality to light through the gospel, [11]for which I was appointed a preacher and apostle and teacher, [12]which is why I suffer as I do. But I am not ashamed, for I know whom I have believed, and I am convinced that he is able to guard until that Day what has been entrusted to me.

(2 Timothy 1:8–12)

We are born with an innate sense of fairness, and it is carefully nurtured if you happen to live in the West.

We come into this world with freedom and liberty infused into our individual DNA, or so it seems. It does not take long for this addiction to fairness to manifest itself. We do not have to teach our children to say "mine" or to insist their rights have been stepped on.

In America, this sense of fairness was written into our founding documents. We earnestly believe we have all been created equal, and we believe this equality means we are all good, valuable, and possessors of certain inalienable rights. With this, I agree, as long as we are talking about who we are as citizens of this world.

When we talk about ourselves as citizens of the spiritual realm, we simply cannot see things the same way. While we all come into this world in the same way, it is not true we are good and valuable and possess a set of rights. In truth, we have inherited a toxin called sin that has pervasively ruined our nature in terms of any ability to please our Creator.

This means any rights we may have had originally, in the mind of our Creator, have now been ruined. According to the Bible, we are dead spiritually, blinded to the truth of God, unwilling and unable to remedy our situation, and are on the path to eternal judgment. What's more, unless something from outside of ourselves comes in with the power to radically change the trajectory of our lives, we are helpless to escape the eternal judgment we all deserve from the hand of Almighty God.

It really does not matter if we think this is unfair. What matters is it is true and the Almighty God and Judge of all will act in perfect justice and holiness to render to us exactly what our rebellious lives and attitudes deserve.

After all, fairness is always defined by justice, and God is unfailingly just. All our rights are defined by him, because we are first and foremost, his creations.

Timothy was toiling in the pagan city of Ephesus, and the work was taking its toll on him. Five years earlier Paul left him there with a charge to establish the church on the platform of truth. Now, having battled the culture for five long years, he was back on his heels, timid, even ashamed of the testimony of Christ. Paul felt compelled to help right his young partner and penned a letter intended to encourage and rejuvenate him. Instead of suggesting a vacation, or some sort of therapeutic exercise, he led him back to the gospel.

The gospel is the good news of God at his best. He is the one who had saved and called Timothy to live and move in holiness. This great rescue from sin, and reformation to righteousness was not affected or merited by Timothy's own works or even his highest aspirations. Rather, God's actions toward Timothy were fueled exclusively by his own grace, according to his grand purpose, which was granted freely and without strings or addendum to Timothy. To amplify the sovereign nature of this wonderful, life-giving gift, Paul declares all this was granted to Timothy in Jesus Christ *from all eternity.*

Can this be? Is Paul really suggesting that, before time even began, God determined to grant Timothy the grace of an effectual rescue from his bondage to sin and a calling to share his holiness? Is Paul suggesting the doctrine of Unconditional Election is a good thing, and is part of the rejuvenating aspect of the gospel? The answer is simply, "Yes that is exactly what Paul is doing."

Notice first, Paul states it clearly without any attempt to shave the edges. He also does not stop to explain or apologize. He simply says God chose Timothy to be a recipient of his saving, sanctifying grace even before God created the first molecules and brought them together to form the earth. This is not an isolated theme for Paul. He had already taught this doctrine to the Ephesians (Eph 1:3–4), reminding them every Christ-follower had been *"chosen in him before the foundation of the world."*

Second, we need to be reminded Paul includes this idea of God's electing love as part of the rejuvenating aspect of the gospel. In the face of spiritual fatigue, Paul reminds Timothy his place in grace is not at risk. Neither his strength nor his weakness can bring about an adjustment to his standing in Christ. Why? Because the matter has been settled — completely — from all eternity.

After all, this whole salvation thing is about God, not us. Our salvation, as well as our sanctification, is a tribute to his power, his love, his wisdom, his gracious disposition toward ruined sinners, and his unfailing love. If any part of our salvation and eventual glorification were dependent upon us, it would only diminish the brightness of his glory.

Lastly, it is important to understand Paul was not making up the idea that God's actions toward us were intellectually complete before time began. He did not fabricate this out of thin air. It was breathed out by God, as is all of Scripture, and Paul complied with it because he knew it to be true.

Paul was quite comfortable, even joyful, at the thought of God's sovereign work in salvation. While the actual accomplishment and application of redemption would take place in time — at the cross, and when we repented and believed — the plan of God was complete, determined, and therefore, guaranteed from all eternity. Let us not forget, this was not Paul's invention. It first comes to the public realm in the teaching of Jesus himself.

In John 6, Jesus is very bold in his explanation of the miraculous feeding of the 5000. Having manipulated and multiplied the molecules of the bread and fish as only the Creator could do, he goes on to explain the truth behind the miracle. He says he has gone one better than Moses, who gave them bread in the wilderness. He has given them bread that will bring about eternal life. This bread of heaven will give life to the world.

Strange as it may seem - some wanted to argue rather than believe. They had seen the miracle, and even eaten the bread, but they still saw Jesus as an enemy rather than the friend they all needed. To their face, Jesus gave the only explanation for such unreasonable behavior on their part:

> [37]All that the Father gives me will come to me, and whoever comes to me I will never cast out. [39]And this is the will of him who sent me, that I should lose nothing of all that he has given me, but raise it up on the last day.
> (John 6:37–39)

The reason they did not believe was they were not part of the group the Father had given to the Son. Jesus goes further in vs. 44: *No one can come to me unless the Father who sent me draws him ...* At this many of the crowd left him. They would not put up with anything that seemed to demean the nobility and freedom of mankind.

At this, Jesus turned to his disciples and asked if this teaching caused them to stumble as well. He asked if they wanted to leave off from following him too. Peter spoke for the group stating that leaving made no sense since Jesus certainly was God's Son, possessor of the words of eternal life:

> [68]"Simon Peter answered him, 'Lord, to whom shall we go? You have the words of eternal life, [69]and we have believed, and have come to know, that you are the Holy One of God.'"
> (John 6:68-69)

Jesus went on to describe the sovereign, electing love of God in Christ in even simpler terms in John 10:14–15, 25–28:

> [14]"I am the good shepherd. I know my own and my own know me, [15]just as the Father knows me and I know the Father; and I lay down my life for the sheep" ... [25]Jesus answered them, "I told you, and you do not believe. The works that I do in my Father's name bear witness about me, [26]but you do not believe because you are not among my sheep. [27]My sheep hear my voice, and I know them, and they follow me. [28]I give them eternal life, and they will never perish, and no one will snatch them out of my hand."

To believe was to give evidence of being "of his sheep", to be numbered among that group chosen in Christ before the foundation of the world (Eph 1:4), to whom grace in Christ had been granted from all eternity (2 Tim 1:9).

Paul had to remind Timothy the work of God in salvation was God's alone. He planned it, he purchased it, he applied it, and Timothy was the recipient of it.

Perhaps, the question remains in our minds: how is this rejuvenating? Isn't the doctrine of God's absolute predestination of all things really a bad thing?

Two problematic questions usually arise at this point:

1) Doesn't it mean we are robots, controlled by some heavenly joystick?

2) And further, doesn't it insinuate we can live any way we want to since nothing can "snatch us out of God's hand?"

The first question, regarding human freedom, always seems to be a thorny issue. Actually, it all depends on what "freedom" really is. Are we really free to do anything we want to do as humans? Actually, no. We cannot fly. As males, we cannot conceive and give birth. In addition, as a bald, old, and short man, I cannot play in the NBA. I have neither the ability nor physique necessary. I have always wanted to. I have had all the will necessary, but simply willing something does not mean the freedom to do it. In reality, freedom is not simply being able to choose what you want to do. Freedom is being able to do what you choose to do. Freedom of the will is actually better understood as the freedom to put into action what you will, or choose to do.

This definition of freedom then, is quite compatible with the truth of God's sovereignty over all things, even our individual lives. Here is how: If my actions grow out of my choices, then I am free and responsible for them. If, however, I am forced to do what I did not choose to do, or if I am restrained from doing what I choose to do, then my freedom has been constrained. If I make a decision to act, and then act accordingly, the act is considered free since it is the fruit of my own mind's decision.

If we take a step back from this process of choice and action, we can easily understand the sovereignty of God as it collides with our ability to choose as free moral agents. Simply put, God is able to bring about our choices, and thus, our actions in ways completely unfelt by us. Whenever we are able to do what we choose to do, we have acted freely, and are accountable for our actions. Is it not true that we do not feel compelled or forced as we go about making our choices every day?

Just how the sovereign plan of God actually intersects with our choices so we act according to his predetermined plan while still feeling and recognizing our actions are our own, is not known. This does not in any way undermine its validity.

To the second question — the issue of being able to live any way we want to — the answer is, surprisingly, yes! You are free to live however you want to! However, if you have truly been overwhelmed by the grace of God in Christ and his Spirit is in you, your "want to" is changing. Through the Spirit and the Word, you are coming more and more to hate sin and love righteousness. You are transitioning from a self-centered consumer to a joyful servant, intent on pleasing and magnifying the glory of the One to whom you owe everything, and from whom you have gained everything.

The apostle John spoke to this very issue in 1 John 3:4–10:

> [4]Everyone who makes a practice of sinning also practices lawlessness; sin is lawlessness. [5]You know that he appeared in order to take away sins, and in him, there is no sin. [6]No one who abides in him keeps on sinning; no one who keeps on sinning has either seen him or known him. [7]Little children, let no one deceive you. Whoever practices righteousness is righteous, as he is righteous. [8]Whoever makes a practice of sinning is of the devil, for the devil has been sinning from the beginning. The reason the Son of God appeared was to destroy the works of the devil. [9]No one born of God makes a practice of sinning, *for God's seed abides in him,* and he cannot keep on sinning because he has been born of God. [10]By this it is evident who are the children of God, and who are the children of the devil: whoever does not practice righteousness is not of God, nor is the one who does not love his brother.

Notice the reason Christ-followers will not live lives characterized by sin is the presence of *"God's seed"* abiding in them. Those in Christ have God the Spirit dwelling in them. This "seed" means they will more and more delight in obedience over sin, and even if sin becomes habitual, the discipline of God will bring them back, for the call of God on their lives is to holiness. The writer of Hebrews (12:5–10) reminds us all of God the Father's loving and consistent discipline for this very purpose:

> [5]"And have you forgotten the exhortation that addresses you as sons? " My son, do not regard

lightly the discipline of the Lord, nor be weary when reproved by him. [6]For the Lord disciplines the one he loves, and chastises every son whom he receives." [7]It is for discipline that you have to endure. God is treating you as sons. For what son is there whom his father does not discipline? [8]If you are left without discipline, in which all have participated, then you are illegitimate children and not sons. [9]Besides this, we have had earthly fathers who disciplined us and we respected them. Shall we not much more be subject to the Father of spirits and live? [10]For they disciplined us for a short time as it seemed best to them, but he disciplines us for our good, that we may share his holiness."

Can we live anyway we want to? For the believer, that is a tricky question simply because the indwelling Spirit of God is transforming our "want to's" through the Word. The freedom we should be most interested in, and thankful for, is the freedom we now have to love God from the heart.

To be in Christ is to be free to love God as we were originally created to do. And I know what you're thinking: It just doesn't seem fair that we could receive from God all Christ has to offer even though we just don't deserve it. I know ... it does not seem fair, but God's love and justice have been satisfied in Christ and in him, we have it all, fair and square.

Perhaps you have taken up this book because you've noticed your "want to's" have been drifting back to the selfishness and sin that once characterized your living. Maybe you have seen the ill effects of that drifting on your relationship with God and with others. Could it be you need some time to reflect on the monumental truth of the gospel? Why not take some time to pray right now. If you are wondering where to start let me make a simple suggestion. Pray through Ephesians 2:1–10 as printed below. Just begin reading and pray along the lines of Paul's magnificent depiction of your rescue from sin into the salvation found only in Jesus Christ.

Let me help you get started …

[1]"And you were dead in the trespasses and sins [2]in which you once walked, following the course of this world, following the prince of the power of the air, the spirit that is now at work in the sons of disobedience— [3]among whom we all once lived in the passions of our flesh, carrying out the desires of the body and the mind, and were by nature children of wrath, like the rest of mankind.

Gracious Father, it has been a long time since I acknowledged what a desperate mess my life was before you opened my eyes to you! And now, thinking about those days, I must admit some of the old thoughts and ways have once again found a place in my heart, and Lord …

[4]But God, being rich in mercy, because of the great love with which he loved us, [5]even when we were dead in our trespasses, made us alive together with Christ— by grace you have been saved— [6]and raised us up with him and seated us with him in the heavenly places in Christ Jesus, [7]so that in the coming ages he might show the immeasurable riches of his grace in kindness toward us in Christ Jesus.

Oh yes Father, I remember when you opened my eyes to my sin, and drew me to Jesus! I remember the joy, the relief, the tears of repentance and faith ... and today I acknowledge just how much I need you, as my God, my Savior! Forgive me Lord, for ...

[8]For by grace you have been saved through faith. And this is not your own doing; it is the gift of God, [9]not a result of works, so that no one may boast. [10]For we are his workmanship, created in Christ Jesus for good works, which God prepared beforehand, that we should walk in them."

(Your turn)

12

NOW APPEARING
... JESUS CHRIST

⁸Therefore do not be ashamed of the testimony about our Lord, nor of me his prisoner, but share in suffering for the gospel by the power of God, ⁹who saved us and called us to a holy calling, not because of our works but because of his own purpose and grace, which he gave us in Christ Jesus before the ages began, ¹⁰and *which now has been manifested through the appearing of our Savior Christ Jesus*, who abolished death and brought life and immortality to light through the gospel, ¹¹for which I was appointed a preacher and apostle and teacher, ¹²which is why I suffer as I do. But I am not ashamed, for I know whom I have believed, and I am convinced that he is able to guard until that Day what has been entrusted to me
(2 Timothy 1:8–12)

As I have already stated, I am a soccer fanatic. I love the game and everything about it. While many

Americans think soccer is boring given the low scores most matches produce, the truth is it is this built-in sense of delayed gratification that makes the emotional side of soccer so fulfilling.

We watch, wait, and get our hopes up, as the ball is passed with precision down the field. The opportunity for a goal is getting nearer and nearer and then ... well, maybe next time. Each buildup, with increasing tension as the games wears on, creates a slowly expanding desire for success. Then, finally, when the centering pass is made, and deftly handled by the striker who calmly fires the ball into the back of the net, our pent up hopes explode in noisy, fist pumping, exclamation! Okay, sorry. I got a bit carried away just thinking about it.

So there, you have it. The longer hope sits brewing, the greater the joy when at last it is fulfilled. God's plan to rescue, reform, and resonate his glory through his elect was set in stone from all eternity. Now it has come to light in Christ Jesus. Let the noisy, joyous, fist pumping begin!

Perhaps Timothy had forgotten his history. Maybe in all his pastoral work he had been too focused on the present, and had left off marveling about the great faithfulness of God in fulfilling the epic promise of Messiah, the Savior. Paul does not mention the reasons this young pastor had fallen prey to spiritual fatigue, timidity, and burnout. He does not even ask Timothy to give him reasons. He just dives right into the water of Timothy's theological heart and demands he recognize once again the majesty of the gospel. He puts it between Timothy's eyes that the good news must wash over him every day, in manifold ways, lest he become weary, lose heart, and maybe lose his way.

I think Paul would have made a good soccer

announcer. He is really good at explaining the buildup. Notice in verses 9 and 10 Paul carefully explains the "buildup" of God's saving work:

> [9]who saved us and called us to a holy calling, not because of our works but because of his own purpose and grace, which he gave us in Christ Jesus before the ages began, [10]and which now has been manifested through the appearing of our Savior Christ Jesus, who abolished death and brought life and immortality to light through the gospel,
> (2 Timothy 1:9–10)

It starts with God, of course, who has saved and called Timothy with a calling that is holy and demands holiness. This great rescue from sin and Satan has not been fueled by Timothy's grand abilities or personal merit. He cannot take any of the credit simply because the whole of it has been designed in the mind of God, and carried out fully through his own grace. It has been a long buildup.

Since before time began, God has been working his plan, deftly passing the promise from generation to generation, from Abraham through Jacob, through Judah and David, and on down the field of human history to a field just outside Bethlehem.

As we read the story of God's promise in the Old Testament for the first time, there are many instances when we are sure the promise is being completed. First, we see Noah. Certainly here is the "he" of Genesis 3:15, the one through whom the whole world has been cleansed from the toxin of sin by the waters of the flood. As it turns out his shot went wide! Noah was not the Savior; he needed a savior.

Then comes Abraham, running with great promise only to show his own human frailties on so many occasions. So on with Jacob, and Samuel and even the great King David. Time after time the hearts of God's faithful are hopeful only to have fulfillment deferred.

Then, finally, it happens. One day in Jerusalem, John sees a man named Jesus walking across the square, and through the Spirit, he recognizes the One who alone is the fulfillment of the promise. The buildup is happening again, but in a way never before seen. "There he is, the Lamb of God who takes away the sin of the world."

It was to this buildup Paul pointed Timothy when he wrote his salvation and calling were actually granted to him in Christ Jesus before the ages *and now has been manifested through the appearing of our Savior Christ Jesus,* (vs. 9, 10a). Can you hear Paul saying, "Timothy, don't you realize we've been privileged to see the promise fulfilled? All those who came before had hope but we have experienced the joy of fulfillment!"

In some ways, the "dark ages" is a fitting label for all those years preceding the birth of Jesus Christ. The people who lived between Eden and Bethlehem lived in a pretty dense fog. In Isaiah, 9:2 the prophet described their day as the darkness into which, one day, the light of Messiah would shine.

While they lived with knowledge of God's great redemptive promise, they saw it only in the shadows. They watched the great sacrificial system, seeing in it some nuanced previews of God's promised reality, while still wondering just how God would punish sin while redeeming sinners.

They understood one would come with heavenly authority to reclaim and reform what sin had polluted, but just who He would be, and how the task would be accomplished was beyond them. Peter understood their longing as generation after generation lived and died without realizing the promise. He described it in 1 Peter 1:10–11:

> [10]Concerning this salvation, the prophets who prophesied about the grace that was to be yours searched and inquired carefully, [11]inquiring what person or time the Spirit of Christ in them was indicating when he predicted the sufferings of Christ and the subsequent glories.

Peter followed that declaration about the prophets with another incredible assertion that the marvels of Messiah and the redemptive plan were *"things into which angels long to look"* (vs. 12). The prophets and the angels, and the people as well, kept staring longingly into the future but only saw the mists of promise. The reality of fulfillment was all too elusive.

We have all looked forward to things. Maybe it was a party, a vacation, or a tee time. Or maybe it was something really big like going off to college, getting married, or buying our first house. In every case, anticipation and excitement grew stronger as the day grew closer. What if you knew something big — something life changing — was promised but you were not given a specific date? How would you sustain your hope?

Throughout the Old Testament, the people of God held onto the promise. Their prophets carefully studied each progressive layer as God unfolded His Messianic plan. Apparently, the mystery was so engrossing even the angels were captivated.

The whole story of God's promised Messiah and His redemptive plan were like the best novel ever written. It was spellbinding. It grabbed your heart and your mind and just would not let go. It also was elusive to all but the last generation of Old Testament saints. Hebrews 11:39 describes the Old Testament people in this way: "*And all these, though commended through their faith, did not receive what was promised...*"

It certainly seems Paul was intending to remind Timothy of the privileged position he occupied as one who had at last seen the promise fulfilled. Perhaps Paul wanted Timothy to remember those who, having far less knowledge than he, remained steadfast and faithful. They had persevered through much worse circumstances than those confronting Timothy in Ephesus. Perhaps Paul wanted Timothy to remember that others, failing to see God act as they had hoped, gave in to their selfishness and fell into the sins of complacency and despair. Just like Timothy.

Paul tells Timothy that having lived to see Messiah is a huge privilege. No longer does he have to live each day with the mere hope of redemption. He now possesses the undying assurance he has been redeemed. His "someday" has become "this day", and today brings the assurance all the tomorrows can be lived before the face of God as a loved child, fully at home and at rest.

The coming of Jesus Christ in heavenly authority and power was akin to the creation of the sun. The light broke into the darkness, and hope was fulfilled. All God had promised he had now made real. The darkness of death would no longer dominate the spiritual landscape of humanity. Now the light of life had come, bearing witness through an empty grave that life as God intended it was now an eternal reality. Jesus turned on the heavenly spotlights focused on himself, and Paul is shouting to Timothy that he must stop focusing on the situations before him and get back to being enthralled with the Savior who has saved him.

Like Timothy, we are all prone to find our identity in our circumstances. We become the challenges we face, the losses we sustain, and the heartaches we carry. It is all too common even among Christ-followers to seek out and commiserate with others who have suffered in the same way. We enter into relationships based our shared sadness, and in our conversations we rehearse our disappointments repeatedly.

We all know people who, while claiming to be Christ-followers, find their identity is their struggles, their diseases, their victim status, or any of a number of tragic life circumstances. Certainly, we must never marginalize what people have endured nor the ongoing effects of those tragedies on their minds and hearts. The whole point of Jesus Christ is he has brought to light a new way of living. In Christ, we have been born again, and to mentally or emotionally continue to see our identity in what has happened to us is actually to go on living in darkness.

As Christ-followers, the things of this world no longer shape our identity. We are new creatures, born again to eternal life. We are not our own, for God has purchased us, and made us his own. Our lives are "in Christ" and in him alone, we find our true identity.

Those who suffer from past parental injustices will find in God the perfect Father. Those who long for the love of family will find they have been adopted into the family of God. Have you been the victim of lies and deceit? In Christ is the truth of God, sealed for us in the Scriptures. Has disease encircled you? With Paul, we understand that, while the outer body is decaying, our inner person — our redeemed soul — is actually being renewed day by day through the Spirit who lives in us. Have you been rejected, disappointed, disrespected, libeled, beaten, mocked, ridiculed, shunned, forgotten, and humiliated? Jesus Christ knows exactly how that feels, and surrounds you not only with his sympathy, but also with his all-encompassing love, righteousness, and protective power. In him none of that matters. Yes, there may still be scars, but they are now only reminders; they no longer define your reality.

Knowing Timothy was surrounded by the darkness of doubt and despair, Paul reminds him of the light of life in Christ Jesus. Was Timothy beginning to find his identity in the struggles and discouragement of ministry in Ephesus? Was he wading in the waters of self-pity? Did he no longer see himself as a divinely appointed spokesman for the Almighty, but rather as the bruised and beaten victim of overwhelming circumstance?

There is no doubt the whole issue of self-concept is a major factor in our lives today. Just who are we? Are we merely the bundle of consequences the past has produced? If so, do we have to go backward to go forward?

Perhaps like Timothy what we really need is to immerse ourselves in good theology. Timothy needed to go back to the gospel to find him, to see his God, to understand his own great need, and once again find complete rest in his Savior. He needed an identity tune up. He desperately needed to once again embrace the radical nature of his life in Christ. He needed to recognize a dramatic change had taken place when he had been born again into the family of God. He was not who he used to be. Christ, not circumstance, now defined him. While scars and certain harmful patterns of thinking and acting were still present, they could no longer dominate, unless he chose to let them.

All that God had planned before time has now been made visible to us. The gospel shouts we no longer have to walk in darkness. We no longer need to be slaves to sin. Our own sins cannot have mastery over us, and neither can those sins perpetrated against us. We have a new status, a new spiritual DNA, and have been freed from bondage to circumstance. We cannot change the past. In Christ, its eternal consequences have been thwarted, and through his Spirit, we can chart a new course of truth, love, and righteousness.

As we read Paul's words today, it has been almost 2000 years since the goal was reached, the promise fulfilled. We must admit, too often the luster seems to have worn off over time. We have read about it, heard many sermons about it, talked about it, and even celebrated it, but sometimes this familiarity, while not breeding contempt, has certainly created complacency.

With Timothy, we may need a fresh engagement with the miracle of the Incarnation that brought redemption out of God's mind and into the world. In the simplest terms, it demonstrates God's great wisdom, his sovereign power, and his absolute faithfulness. Who but our God could design and accomplish such an intricate plan as "the Word made flesh?" Who but our God could orchestrate human history so the Incarnation happened in just the right way, through just the right people, in just the right place, at just the right time? Who but our God has proven himself faithful over the entirety of human history?

The plan of God has never been derailed, either by the opposition of his enemies or the disobedience of his friends. Our God is unimaginably wise, unassailably strong, and unfailingly faithful.

The incarnation of Jesus has revealed the very nature of God to us even as it has brought into the light of reality the promise of rescue first given in Eden. God's entire buildup of the redemptive plan has been revealed in the appearing of our Savior, Christ Jesus.

Timothy needed to be reminded of this. You and I need to be reminded of this every day as well. May the Lord grant us faithful eyes to see the goodness of his grace in the gospel, for his glory and our daily good.

13

DING, DONG
DEATH IS DEAD

⁸Therefore do not be ashamed of the testimony about our Lord, nor of me his prisoner, but share in suffering for the gospel by the power of God, ⁹who saved us and called us to a holy calling, not because of our works but because of his own purpose and grace, which he gave us in Christ Jesus before the ages began, ¹⁰and which now has been manifested through the appearing of our Savior Christ Jesus, who *abolished death* and brought life and immortality to light through the gospel, ¹¹for which I was appointed a preacher and apostle and teacher, ¹²which is why I suffer as I do. But I am not ashamed, for I know whom I have believed, and I am convinced that he is able to guard until that Day what has been entrusted to me.
(2 Timothy 1:8–12)

Increasingly our society is infatuated with, and plagued by, death. This is incredibly ironic, even paradoxical. We hate it, fear it, and yet we pay millions to see it described and displayed on the big screen. We flock to funerals out of obligation, or to see how the family is fairing, all the while hoping the service does not last more than an hour. Staring death in the face for longer than an hour seems unbearable, especially if the preacher reminds us we will never escape death ourselves.

With death posing a very real threat to our peace of mind, how in the world can Paul declare death has been abolished? Is this some sort of wishful thinking, or an example of theological mythology?

To start with, remember Paul is writing to encourage a young man — Timothy — whose life seemed to be under the cascading waves of adversity. Whatever the circumstances of Timothy's life, he was apparently out of gas, increasingly off in his own corner, and seemingly ashamed of Jesus and the gospel. It appears to have started with an increasing aversion to suffering. Perhaps he recognized societal persecution could eventually mean death, and that was not something he'd signed up for.

Paul determined to hit the problem head on.

Up to this point, the apostle had been reminding Timothy of God the Father's part in the gospel story. He had planned and orchestrated all things to bring about the salvation promised throughout the Old Testament. This glorious plan had now been revealed in the incarnate Word, God the Son, Jesus Christ. The curtain had at last been raised, and the magnificence of Messiah was on full display. Paul insists there is much more to the story.

Not only had Jesus come, fulfilling the hopes, dreams and prophecies of the Old Testament people, but he had also accomplished the monumental task of redemption. When he said, "it is finished!" it really was. Sin was judged. Justice was served. Sinners would now become children of God, and his love would be seen in all its divine grandeur.

There was more to the work of Jesus Christ than the cross.

It is an ironic fact that too often, in our modern gospel telling, we leave Jesus on the cross. We boldly champion his death for the sins of mankind, passionately declaring the love of God the Father and the humility and love of God the Son. We extol the wisdom of the divine plan whereby love and justice are both satisfied through the substitution of Christ for us. We love to use the cross as a symbol of our love for Christ, and our trust in his finished work on our behalf.

All too often, we put the empty grave in the margins, and only bring it out on Resurrection Sunday. Yet, Paul and the apostles would not stand for such a truncated gospel. For them, the resurrection of Jesus Christ is every bit as important as the cross, for without it, nothing would have changed. As Paul clearly shows in his masterful treatise on the importance of the resurrection in 1 Corinthians 15, without the empty grave, *"we are of all people most to be pitied."* Why? Simply because we have deprived ourselves of earthly pleasures based on our faith in Jesus who, without the resurrection, turns out to be just another great teacher and not a Savior.

To do justice to the resurrection would take much more space than we have here. Notice that Paul's purpose was much more focused in his advice to Timothy. He does not go into proofs of the resurrection as he did in 1 Corinthians 15:3–8. Neither does he give a full-orbed explanation of how the resurrection fits into the gospel, or factors into our justification, or validates our faith as he does elsewhere in his epistles. Rather, he centers in on death, and how Jesus Christ ended its terror and reign for all who are "in him."

Years ago I was speaking at a Men's Conference in Washington state and decided to drive from my home in Tacoma. My route took me across the Hood Canal floating bridge, and the scenery all the way was magnificent. Just as I crossed the bridge, my car died. I was out in the country, and living before cell phones so there was no other recourse than to flag down a passing motorist. Providentially, a guy in a big pickup stopped, determined the problem could not be fixed easily, and offered to tow me a few miles to the nearest mechanic's shop. I agreed and he fastened a large chain from his undercarriage to my front bumper. We started on our way.

As we pulled out, I suddenly realized my steering column was locked, and the keys were in my pocket. Unable to steer, I began drifting into the oncoming lane, and looked in terror to see a semi cruising down the hill toward me. In my mind, I panicked. I remember things moving in slow motion, just as I had heard others say but never believed. Somehow, I retrieved the keys, stuck the right one in the ignition, unlocked the column, and was able to steer out of harm's way. It must have taken only seconds but my heart continued pounding for several minutes. To this day, I remember staring death in the face, and it is not something I ever want to do again. But, I know I will, unless Jesus returns before death takes me.

We all fear death. It is a robber that comes inevitably, and steals away our most precious possession. So, what exactly did Paul mean when he said Christ Jesus *abolished death?*

Just this. He was reminding Timothy and every reader since that day, what life and death really are. Death can be defined as the cessation of bodily life. That would not be a full definition in God's eyes. Ever since Adam and Eve ate the forbidden fruit and died, we've understood God's definition of death as no longer being acceptable to him, no longer being connected to the fullness of life found only in him. While the first couple continued existing, breathing, and living out their days in the flesh, in terms of spiritual life, they were dead. They were dead in their sins, and only God could regenerate them, and bring them back into life indeed.

Even before the incarnation, new life was based on the finished work of Christ. It was previewed in the sacrificial system of Israel, and apprehended by faith in God's promise of the "he" of Genesis 3:15 who would turn curse into blessing. From the beginning, God granted new life to those who trusted in him alone to fix the "death" problem sin created.

Throughout Old Testament history, it was the sacrificial system that pointed to God as the only means of salvation. The blood of bulls and goats and lambs signified the promise of God to one day overcome the corruption of sin forever. The blood of animals could "cover" sin for a time, but it could never take it away. Even when practiced, the sacrifices themselves held the ever-present knowledge that sin was part of human existence. It was a relentless disease, and God's promise held the only remedy.

The resurrection accomplished many things. First, it validated the entire incarnational plan, including Jesus' deity. It established Jesus as our great High Priest, now seated at the right hand of God where he constantly intercedes for his own. It fulfilled the Old Testament prophecies of David, as well as those of Jesus himself regarding the eternality of Messiah and the fact that death would never hold him. I could go on and on. Paul's point is clear. He simply wanted Timothy to remember Jesus abolished death, denying its power over humanity, and forever releasing his redeemed ones from its terror and bondage.

The writer of Hebrews put it very well, in Hebrews 2:14–15:

> [14]"Since therefore the children share in flesh and blood, he himself likewise partook of the same things, that through death he might destroy the one who has the power of death, that is, the devil, [15]and deliver all those who through fear of death were subject to lifelong slavery."

To abolish death — that sin-driven separation from God — was to forever banish the effects of sin. This Jesus did, completely and eternally on the cross. Those who are "in Christ" can never return to the state of spiritual death simply because it has, for them, been abolished. Once we enter into spiritual life through the transforming grace of God, our former state is no longer possible. The one who died for us now lives for us, and our position in him is eternally secure.

Wait, there is even more! Not only did Jesus Christ abolish the possibility of devolving back into a state of spiritual death for those who believe, he also forever inoculated us against the fear of physical death by declawing Satan, the great enemy of God.

Death, as the consequence of sin, had always been the most powerful weapon in Satan's arsenal. When the stone was rolled away, and Jesus walked out alive, death itself was overwhelmed and forever removed as a threat to those for whom he had died.

For those "in Christ" death was transformed from an event that ends life into the inauguration of that perfect, sinless life lived in unobstructed fellowship with our God. While we may still fear the pain and diminished capacity that often accompany the last years of our temporal lives, death itself must hold no fear for the Christ-followers.

Why? Because, as Paul tells us, the removal of our physical body — either by death or miraculous change at the coming of Christ — is a necessary event if we are to inhabit the kingdom of God in its fullness.

Remember what Paul said? *50"I tell you this, brothers: flesh and blood cannot inherit the kingdom of God, nor does the perishable inherit the imperishable. 51Behold! I tell you a mystery. We shall not all sleep, but we shall all be changed, 52in a moment, in the twinkling of an eye, at the last trumpet. For the trumpet will sound, and the dead will be raised imperishable, and we shall be changed."* (1 Corinthians 15:50–52)

In order to experience the inheritance we have in Christ it is necessary for our fleshly bodies to be removed and replaced.

For the great majority of Christ-followers this will mean physical death and resurrection. Only those alive when Christ returns will escape physical death. In either case, death no longer poses a horrible mystery. For believers, it is God's divine way to dress us for life eternal.

If the seed of Timothy's despair, reticence, and spiritual fatigue was his fear of suffering, Paul's words were a reminder that this life is not the end. It is only the prelude to the next life, and is to be lived in light of our eternal inheritance. In this world, we may experience tribulation, trial, pain, and tragedy. God has promised the adversity of this life is miniscule compared to the eternal glory we will know, the peace we will enjoy, and the delight we will experience with God on a new earth where only righteousness will dwell.

Paul summed it all up with these encouraging words:

> [13]Since we have the same spirit of faith according to what has been written, "I believed, and so I spoke," we also believe, and so we also speak, [14]knowing that he who raised the Lord Jesus will raise us also with Jesus and bring us with you into his presence. [15]For it is all for your sake, so that as grace extends to more and more people it may increase thanksgiving, to the glory of God. [16]So we do not lose heart. Though our outer self is wasting away, our inner self is being renewed day by day. [17]For this light, momentary affliction is preparing for us an eternal weight of glory beyond all comparison, [18]as we look not to the things that are seen but to the things that are unseen. For the things that are seen are transient, but the things that are unseen are eternal. (2 Cor. 4:13–18)

14

TURN ON YOUR
LIFE LIGHT

[8]Therefore do not be ashamed of the testimony about our Lord, nor of me his prisoner, but share in suffering for the gospel by the power of God, [9]who saved us and called us to a holy calling, not because of our works but because of his own purpose and grace, which he gave us in Christ Jesus before the ages began, [10]and which now has been manifested through the appearing of our Savior Christ Jesus, who abolished death and *brought life and immortality to light* through the gospel, [11]for which I was appointed a preacher and apostle and teacher, [12]which is why I suffer as I do. But I am not ashamed, for I know whom I have believed, and I am convinced that he is able to guard until that Day what has been entrusted to me.
(2 Timothy 1:8–12)

As I mentioned before, I was privileged to grow up in a pastor's family. My dad was a solid biblical expositor with a shepherd's heart. Although my life was not captured by Christ until my high school years, the truth and morality of the Bible were all around me. Church and God and Jesus formed the wallpaper of my life, and while it seemed oppressive at the time, I have come to greatly appreciate all God had for me during my growing up years.

I have some strange memories of church life however. One year an evangelist came to town with a special skill that really packed the place. He would set an easel and canvas on our little church stage and begin preaching. As he preached, he also used chalk to draw a picture that went along with his sermon. I was fascinated. Night after night, I would sit in the front row to watch as he hurriedly sketched, drew, and colored a different masterpiece. It was neither the sermon nor the picture that held my attention. It was the ending!

As both the drawing and the sermon came to a close, he would ask for the house lights to be dimmed as he placed a black light over the picture. Suddenly a completely new image would appear.

One I particularly remember was the sermon on hell. The drawing was scary, with flames and darkness creating a haunting image. When the black light hit it, Jesus was standing there in bright, white clothes, radiating salvation. I can remember that shocking moment as though it were yesterday. I am not advocating for shock chalk evangelism, but it sure was cool to all my grade school friends and me.

The memory is etched on my mind for many reasons, but primarily because something hidden suddenly became visible, and it changed the whole picture. I think that is what Paul meant when he declared triumphantly to Timothy that, in Jesus Christ, *life and immortality were brought to light!*

As we have listened to Paul's wonderful review of God's sovereign plan to save and sanctify a people for his own possession, it has been clear, life and immortality have always been there, in the mind of God. In some respects, they were hidden. Beginning in Genesis 3:15 God promised one day a "he" would arise to set things right again. At the time, what "right," meant was not known. It was hidden.

In Jesus Christ, the mystery of God's intention for the world has been cleared up. As we have seen, in Christ, life as God always intended it, can be experienced eternally. The mortal puts on immortality and is fitted for eternity.

Yet, it seems redundant for Paul to say this again. After all, he has already exclaimed everything has been manifested in the appearance of Jesus Christ on the stage of history. Why say it again?

Perhaps Paul is aiming at Timothy's circumstances specifically, and at ours as we fall into the same distressing waters that were overwhelming him. Remember, Timothy was seemingly afraid of suffering for the gospel. Like us all, he had no desire for distress, much less physical abuse, and pain.

Whatever the specific reasons, Timothy was paying much more attention to his mortality than the reality of his immortal soul. He was living more in the realm of the physical than the spiritual. It appears he was more concerned about dying than living, more interested in caring for his mortal body than rejoicing in the immortality found in Christ. He had forgotten where the real light of life was located.

Sometimes we just need a reminder that Jesus has brought life and immortality to light, in the gospel, and in our lives. As those chalk drawings, sometimes what we see at first is not what actually matters most. Sure, our world is broken, and our days filled with circumstances that sometimes discourage and hurt us. What do we expect in a world where sin had corrupted its operating system, and our Enemy is roaming around like a hungry lion? Too often, we become preoccupied with our problems, and too fixated on our own abilities to withstand and overcome them. To do so is to forget where the light is really shining.

If we could turn a "black light" on our lives as Christ-followers we would see our Lord Christ standing in the middle of everyday, no matter the chaos, no matter the circumstance, no matter the pain. He will never forsake us, and promises always to use all things to shape us according to his good plan. His goal is to make us like Jesus, to fit us for usefulness in this life, and magnificent happiness in the next.

Wherever you are today, whether walking the high road of delight in Christ, trudging through the valley of despair, or somewhere in between, just know the light of life in Christ is never dimmed except as we close our eyes to it. In him, we have the light of life, and the promise of immortality, no matter how dark the day may seem.

15

THE REVELATION OF LIFE

⁸Therefore do not be ashamed of the testimony about our Lord, nor of me his prisoner, but share in suffering for the gospel by the power of God, ⁹who saved us and called us to a holy calling, not because of our works but because of his own purpose and grace, which he gave us in Christ Jesus before the ages began, ¹⁰and which now has been manifested through the appearing of our Savior Christ Jesus, who abolished death and brought life and immortality to light *through the gospel,* ¹¹for which I was appointed a preacher and apostle and teacher, ¹²which is why I suffer as I do. But I am not ashamed, for I know whom I have believed, and I am convinced that he is able to guard until that Day what has been entrusted to me.

(2 Timothy 1:8–12)

If we look back at the text we've been studying we'll see Paul has used the word "gospel" to bookend his overview of God's saving plan. He starts his review of God's redemptive work in vs. 8 with his exhortation to *"suffer for the gospel,"* and ends it here in vs. 10 declaring *"life and immortality"* were brought to light *"through the gospel."*

For Paul, the gospel was essential. He uses this word as an overall description of God's entire redemptive plan over 70 times in his letters. It was never simply a label. For Paul, the gospel was life and life giving. Accordingly, he applies it to Timothy's soul as the most powerful spiritual medicine ever.

What caused Timothy's reticence is never described. Its effects are clear. Timothy's reluctance made it look as though he was ashamed of the gospel out of fear that boldness would bring suffering. This struck at the heart of Paul's passion and ministry. Paul could never allow such behavior to go uncontested.

Paul left Timothy in Ephesus with specific instructions to teach the truth and confront those who taught otherwise (see: 1 Timothy 1:3–7). Now five years later, Timothy was back on his heels, and the church was suffering. The great needs were a recovery of the mission and a rejuvenation of the missionary.

This Paul does with great simplicity: *Timothy, the very gospel you are ashamed of is the glorious message of Jesus Christ through whom death has been abolished, and life and immortality brought to light! This message is yours to live in, yours to preach, yours to wield as the only cure for sin and death.*

In two short verses, Paul gives a stirring summary of the gospel. In fact, it is more than a summary; it is a glorious presentation. In the gospel, Paul saw much more than an introductory message to Christianity. He saw it as much more than "first things." The gospel must not be relegated to the kindergarten of Christian education as though this essential story, with all its complexity, could be mastered easily and left behind in favor of greater, weightier issues.

For Paul the gospel was the great foundation, fuel, purpose, and goal of life. Everything he did was shaped and sustained by the gospel. Nothing else had any purpose for Paul. No other message or motivation moved him. His very life, right down to the daily risks he often faced, was his response to the call of God to own, trust, obey, and proclaim the gospel.

This gave Paul great insight into Timothy's life. His gaze was penetrating. He saw past the presenting problems Timothy described. I can imagine Pastor Timothy complained about how hard ministry was in Ephesus.

He most certainly had his share of problem people, obstinate mockers, religious persecutors, and financial shortfalls. Like every pastor, he surely suffered from weekly bouts of doubt, fatigue, and the sense that none of his efforts were really accomplishing much. Paul saw through it all.

Not for a minute did Paul try to give Timothy ministry advice. That would come later. He did not point him to the latest book on worship styles or staff organization or mission. He did not recommend any special conferences or pastoral burnout retreats. What he did was remind him simply but powerfully that, at the very core of his calling, was the privilege to understand and proclaim the gospel.

It was very simple: Timothy needed the gospel to once again squeeze the breath of temporal circumstances out of him so he could inhale the majesty, beauty, and power of God. He needed the clarity and comfort that only the gospel — rightly known and preached in the heart — could bring.

Using "gospel" as a pair of bookends, Paul powerfully brought out Timothy's core challenge. He was afraid to live a conspicuously gospel-centered, holiness-characterized, and light-shining life because he did not fully understand, embrace, and rest in the essential elements of the grand gospel of God. It is that simple.

Yes, Timothy had faith, and once had a passion for life and service. That flame died down for lack of daily fuel. That passion faded from lack of daily delight in the wonders of God's sovereignty, holiness, truth, and love. Timothy may have begun living for God, and ministering for Christ, but he had forgotten the primary importance of living with God in terms of a robust, daily relationship grounded in the finished work of Jesus Christ. Paul's remedy was simply to pull him back from his fears to find rest and refuge in the garden of grace we know as the gospel.

As we have walked with Paul through these few verses, we have seen clearly that the gospel has a breadth and depth not usually associated with the word "gospel" in our day. Our gospel has been downsized. Consequently, our evangelism has been marginalized. We have become "production oriented" and are in love with expediency. Our evangelistic efforts have focused on getting people to agree to the minimum amount of truth about God necessary to gain entrance to heaven. Like buying a ticket for the train, we are trying to sell sinners passage to glory at the lowest price.

Ask most Christ-followers today what the "gospel" is and they may cite 1 Corinthians 15:3,4 as though the historical certainty of the death, burial, and resurrection of Christ exhausts the gospel. Others might be able to give four memorized sentences meant to walk the unbeliever from ruined sinner to converted saint. Still others might suggest the gospel is the good news that God loves sinners and wants to spend eternity with as many as he can.

All these certainly have truth in them. Yet it remains a pervasive obstacle to the gospel cause that so many are so ignorant of so much of what the gospel really is.

In the verses we have been considering, we find Paul's gospel spans history from before time began, to the present. It is the story of God's sovereign and gracious plan to rescue what sin has corrupted, reforming it into lives that radiate his glory. This plan provided the God-man, Jesus Christ, in whom and through whom the plan of the Triune God was brought to light. In the person and accomplishments of Jesus, the redemptive plan entered into human history with heavenly authority and eternal purpose.

Through the gospel message, this plan continues today toward its grand conclusion. God is collecting, changing, and empowering a people for his own name, to demonstrate and declare his glory. He is their God. Jesus is their Lord. The Spirit is their teacher and guide.

Fortunately, there are many who understand the gospel in these terms. More and more the gospel is being seen as a broader story that encompasses God's working from Eden on. This trend is very encouraging. We are seeing a reaffirmation of Paul's insistence that, in the gospel, we have God's revelation of life.

There remains a second blind spot in the evangelical world. We too quickly assume the gospel is primarily for those who have not yet entrusted their lives to Jesus. Too often, we link the gospel to the work of evangelism and consider the primary audience of this great story to be unbelievers. Those who have already believed it and been secured by God through it also need to hear it and revel in it often.

Timothy's slide into timidity can be traced to his lack of intentional reflection on the miraculous message of the gospel. Paul thought it essential for Timothy to be plunged into the gospel stream as a regular discipline. It is essential that every Christ-follower let that same stream wash over them regularly.

For all of us living in the jumble of ultra-modernity, there remains an especially urgent, daily need for the gospel. The society we inhabit is increasingly delighting in its declaration that truth is relative, morality is flexible, identity is fluid, and atheism is laudable. In the midst of this tidal wave of change, Christ-followers are charged with living lives conspicuous for their holiness, obedience, sacrificial love, and robust gospel proclamation.

To do all this well we need to know God in deeper and fuller ways. We need to focus our hearts away from the pursuit of self-esteem in order to build greater Christ-esteem. We need to recognize the myth that our temporal circumstances are what shape our identity and rest daily and powerfully in the glorious truth that our identity is found in Christ alone.

Our culture will not like this of course. Our neighbors, both inside and outside the church, want us to continue with them in a Christianity that makes way for the preferences and formulas of our culture. This is not what Jesus wants. He wants us for his own. He wants all of us, every part and the whole of us. He wants our attention and our intentions. He wants our thoughts and our ideas. He wants our goals and our strategies, our ambitions and our successes. He wants what is rightfully his, and having been bought out of slavery and transferred into his keeping, we belong to him in our entirety.

I can imagine Timothy knew all this, and it scared him. After all, he had dreams, plans, and ambition. He wanted to do great things for God, but probably like us, also wanted some benefit, some recognition, and some applause. We are all like that. We are all prone to think about ourselves even when pursuing what we think is best for God. Fortunately, Paul saw right past the facade and into the core of Timothy's heart. What he saw needed fixing.

For Timothy and for us, the solution is always the gospel. When the circumstances of life start trying to mold our identity or sense of worth, the gospel reminds us where our true worth lies.

When the successes of this world inflate our self-importance the gospel reminds us who we really are. And when opposition or fatigue or disappointment whisper in our ears and we start to listen, remember … in the gospel our true story is still being told by the One who has saved us and called us to holiness in order to demonstrate through us the grandeur of his power and grace.

16

A ROYAL APPOINTMENT

⁸Therefore do not be ashamed of the testimony about our Lord, nor of me his prisoner, but share in suffering for the gospel by the power of God, ⁹who saved us and called us to a holy calling, not because of our works but because of his own purpose and grace, which he gave us in Christ Jesus before the ages began, ¹⁰and which now has been manifested through the appearing of our Savior Christ Jesus, who abolished death and brought life and immortality to light through the gospel, ¹¹*for which I was appointed a preacher and apostle and teacher,* ¹²which is why I suffer as I do. But I am not ashamed, for I know whom I have believed, and I am convinced that he is able to guard until that Day what has been entrusted to me.

(2 Timothy 1:8–12)

Many years ago, a man approached me in our church that I did not know very well. He said he wanted some time, and being somewhat new to the pastoral position, I went ahead and set up an appointment without asking the right questions. When we met, I knew within minutes he saw this as a sales call, and not a time of spiritual discussion. He informed me he was a financial advisor, had just finished a two-week course in such matters, and was certain he could help me in many areas. I remember having to stifle my laughter. I felt sorry for him actually, since he seemed sincere in believing a two-week course could make him an expert. Ultimately, he left my office disappointed.

When Paul took on the challenge of helping Timothy he did not do it as a novice, or as an ivory tower academic who merely read and wrote on the subject. He spoke from a platform of Christian experience, and battle-hardened expertise. The obstacles, challenges, and failures Timothy had met face-to-face were not unique. Paul knew them all, inside and out, front and back. Paul was a veteran of the spiritual wars that continually swirled around those champions of Christ who, clothed in his righteousness, were roaming the darkness as agents of light and life. Yes, he had been rescued from the domain of darkness and transferred into the kingdom of God's dear Son, in whom he had redemption, the forgiveness of sins (Colossians 1:13–14). Now, outfitted with the armor of God and the gospel, Paul had been commissioned back into the realm of brokenness as an agent of rescue. That commission meant a life-long commitment.

Timothy was just beginning his commitment, and the inner cry to quit and run was increasingly powerful. For whatever reason, he was losing his courage. He seemed unwilling to suffer for a gospel of which he was increasingly ashamed.

Not so the Apostle. Paul believed he had a divine calling, a royal appointment. Having been rescued by the gospel, he was now convinced both of its power and his charge to be its messenger. You can hear his voice fill with honor as he shouts, *"Of this gospel I have been appointed a preacher, and an apostle and a teacher."* In great contrast to Timothy's increasing desire to throw off the obligations of such a calling, Paul stands tall and declares the nobility of being a spokesman for Jesus Christ.

Paul knew no greater honor that to be a preacher, a spokesman, and a herald. The Greek word translated *preacher* (khvrux, kerux) denoted a man employed by a government or military official to whom was entrusted the proclamation of official news to the public. This herald had a very simple task: take the message of his master, in the authority of the master, and deliver it without compromise.

Paul reveled in the fact that, though he considered himself of all men most sinful, he had been called not only to life in Christ, but also to a position as Christ's herald. He now spoke for the King who had rescued him from the sin and wrath he deserved. He was now a highly placed recruiter for the very beliefs he once persecuted to death.

Too often, we think of people like Paul and Timothy as the only ones commissioned to take the gospel of Jesus Christ to the world. The truth remains each Christ-follower is meant to be a billboard for the truth of God's sovereign grace.

You may not have been appointed to an official office in the church, but, if you are a Christ-follower, you have been called to partner with Jesus Christ in the greatest rescue mission ever. It is not supposed to be a burden. After all, God is the one who saves, and he does so through the gospel. All we have to do is carry it with us, and declare it through both our lives and our lips.

Everyday God is in the process of drawing people to Jesus. Everyday it is our privilege to intersect with some of them, although we may not know just who they are. We find ways to make contacts and friends in the normal rhythms of life, offering the gospel in bits and stages in hopes the Spirit will ride in on the truth and do a transforming work.

Maybe you picked up this book because you have been discouraged or overwhelmed with the "stuff" of life. Possibly, you have felt this way for some time. Have you noticed yourself being angry or critical more often? Do you find the challenges you face becoming increasingly the focus of your thinking and reflection? If so, I hope what you have read has been a good correction, even a comfort. Even as you are attempting to find rest and refuge in the garden of grace that is the gospel, there is one more thing you need to consider.

The redeemed life was never supposed to be self-focused. Christ never called us to himself only to have us become content to think only of ourselves. While it may be difficult to understand, any preoccupation with self that keeps us from focusing on Christ is ultimately self-defeating. When we allow our minds to fixate on our circumstances, we actually isolate and insulate ourselves from the spiritual power we need to press through them to find delight in Christ and satisfaction in his mission.

We have been called away from the things of this broken world to find contentment, honor, and purpose in the glorious adventure of seeing lives transformed through the gospel. It turns out to be a zero sum game of sorts. To the extent our vision is away from self and focused on Christ, the things of this world — both good and bad — will fade in significance. The converse is true as well. When our minds are filled with personal concerns, wrongs suffered, adverse situations, and the pains of life, it will bring out the worst in us, and others will notice. As Christ-followers, we will experience the most contentment, the most happiness, and the most satisfaction when we are focused on Christ and striving to follow him closely, wherever he leads and whatever the circumstance.

That was Paul's attitude, and he passionately challenged Timothy to break out of his selfishness to once again see the light, walk the life, and take refuge in the strong tower of God's redeeming love known as the gospel.

17

AND SO WE SUFFER UNASHAMED

⁸Therefore do not be ashamed of the testimony about our Lord, nor of me his prisoner, but share in suffering for the gospel by the power *of God, ⁹who saved us* and called us to a holy calling, not because of our works but because of his own purpose and grace, which he gave us in Christ Jesus before the ages began, ¹⁰and which now has been manifested through the appearing of our Savior Christ Jesus, who abolished death and brought life and immortality to light through the gospel, ¹¹for which I was appointed a preacher and apostle and teacher, ¹²*which is why I suffer as I do. But I am not ashamed, for I know whom I have believed, and I am convinced that he is able to guard until that Day what has been entrusted to me.*

(2 Timothy 1:8–12)

At Grace Baptist Church, where I am privileged to be part of the pastoral team, we have a simple sentence that defines the most important thing we do here. When we look at everything we attempt as a church, there is one thing we must do well in order for all the others to coalesce together to accomplish our mission of "making and multiplying Christ-followers who magnify the glory of God."

We put it this way. *In order to accomplish our mission we must teach and model God's Word, in the power of the Spirit, engaging our world as agents of transformation.*

It is important to us that we do not stop at simply teaching God's Word, although it is both primary and essential. It is just as important for us to model what we teach. Evidently, Paul would have agreed.

After calling Timothy back to a robust appreciation of, and daily reflection on the gospel, Paul goes on to show how he has remained unashamed, and willing to suffer for the cause of Christ. What he was calling Timothy to, he had consistently practiced. Paul was not simply a teacher. He both taught and modeled God's truth.

Unlike Timothy, Paul saw suffering as part of the package. Did his call as a herald put him in situations where the audience would not appreciate his message? So, be it! Paul was neither ashamed of his Master, nor the message entrusted to him. Did it invite reprisals and even persecution? Bring it on! No amount of suffering could dissuade him from his absolute commitment to the One whose grace had eternally changed the trajectory of his life. Once bound for God's wrath, he was now saved by God's grace, and was passionate about being used for God's glory.

There was one more thing Paul wanted Timothy to resolve in him. The message Timothy was increasingly ashamed of was the very one in which he had placed his eternal hope. Jesus Christ was the safe into which Paul and Timothy had deposited their lives. Despite all the challenges, heartache, and suffering connected with the gospel ministry, Paul needed Timothy to understand one thing: The Jesus they preached was also the Jesus in whom they had invested everything. Is he able to fulfill the promise of eternal life? Is he trustworthy? On the other hand, was Timothy thinking that maybe another offer held more promise?

Paul finishes the argument with a solid declaration: Jesus Christ can and must be trusted. Paul knew Christ. He did not just know about him; he knew him. What he had come to know and experience gave him rock solid assurance that Jesus Christ was able to keep all his promises.

No need to be ashamed of Jesus. No need to look elsewhere for salvation. No need to abandon the gospel to avoid suffering. Jesus Christ, the Lord of all had their lives firmly in his hands. He is the Able One. We are to find our rest in him.

So ends Paul's brief but powerful admonition to young Timothy. From here the letter goes on to encourage the young pastor to be strong, an unashamed workman that cuts the Scriptures straight, fully prepared to stand firm during the bad times which are just around the corner. All of this was predicated on the renewal of Timothy's soul. To do this, Paul took his cue from the God of Elijah in 1 Kings 18 and 19.

You will remember that Elijah came on the scene when the northern kingdom of Israel was at its lowest, most wicked point. The culture had been taken over by idolatry and paganism. God's people had forsaken him for Baal. They had come to worship Baal, and more to the point, they were intoxicated with the immorality and wickedness the worship of Baal allowed them. They had left their God and the ways of righteousness behind to dwell in the tents of wickedness.

To demonstrate their folly and the validity of Yahweh, Elijah challenged the prophets of Baal to an amazing duel on top of Mt. Carmel, (chronicled in 1 Kings 18). When God sent fire from heaven, Elijah won the biggest battle of his life. He had just watched his God accomplish the greatest miracle of the day. It was to be Elijah's finest hour.

The next day found Elijah running south, all the way to the Negev, afraid for his life. God found him there and listened to his pathetic wishes to die since he felt he was no better than his fathers were. He had failed to unite the tribes. He had failed to rid the land of idolaters. He had failed to incite the people to throw off the wicked reign of Ahab and Jezebel. God had other plans. He set about to rejuvenate the prophet and send him back to his life with purpose.

In an amazing demonstration, God took Elijah back to the basics. He took him to Sinai. It was on Sinai God first revealed his glory and his truth to Moses. It was on Sinai Moses really came to know God, to see him in all his glory, power, and grace. It was on Sinai Moses was transformed from a goat herder to God's leader, the great prophet who would communicate the law of God to the people of God. Therefore, it was on Sinai God brought Elijah back to the fundamentals, back to a reliance on his power and a commitment to his plan. After Sinai, Elijah re-entered his life of ministry for God, no longer afraid, no longer paralyzed by personal pride, and no longer running away from the tasks God had called him to perform.

In a similar way, Paul took Timothy back to the mountain. In this case, the mountain of beginnings was the gospel of Jesus Christ. It is in the gospel we see God revealed in all his glory and truth. It is in the gospel we really come to know God and his Son, Jesus. It is through the gospel our blind eyes are opened and we come to see the reality of our sin and the unimaginable beauty of grace. It is through the gospel God's life is imparted and our souls are set on the path of transformation. The gospel is the mountain that clarifies everything. Paul took Timothy to the mountain, and like Elijah, he heard the still small voice of God calling him back to trust, back to diligence, back to the vitality needed to accomplish the mission.

The mountain of the gospel is still standing, still powerful, still available. Take your weary soul up the mountain and find rest in the garden of grace that is the gospel.

APPENDIX

● ▬ ● ▬ ●

18 USES OF
THE GOSPEL

¹³Follow the pattern of the sound words that you have heard from me, in the faith and love that are in Christ Jesus. ¹⁴By the Holy Spirit who dwells within us, guard the good deposit entrusted to you.
(2 Timothy 1:13–14)

As Paul exhorted Timothy to guard the "good deposit," the gospel in his day, there remains a need for all who follow Christ to *retain* and *guard* that same treasure today. This means much more than merely knowing and loving the good news. It means preaching it to ourselves as well as using it as the foundation of what we think and do. The gospel is not a museum piece to be praised and polished. It is a great tool kit containing so many valuable tools for maintaining vitality and fidelity in our theology, our personal lives, and the ministry of the church.

The ways in which the gospel can be used in our lives as Christ-followers probably number in the thousands. It would be a worthy discipline for us all to make our own list and in this way keep mindful of the ongoing power of the gospel in the life of the believer.

The following thoughts may be helpful in beginning your own list. I have compiled a compact set of things the gospel tells us about our God, ourselves, and the mission of the church.

THE GOSPEL TELLS US ABOUT THE GOD WE SERVE:

1. IT DEMONSTRATES THE NATURE OF GOD

The gospel teaches us about the nature of the God we proclaim: His sovereignty, His generosity, His sensitivity, His great love, and His eternal faithfulness.

2. IT DECLARES THE REDEMPTIVE PLAN OF GOD

The gospel continually reminds us of God's greatness in perfectly superintending his redemptive plan. That plan is proceeding right on time and will absolutely reach its intended goal.

3. IT FOCUSES ON THE GLORY OF GOD

The gospel will keep us ever mindful that God's glory alone is the grand purpose and goal of all creation. We are saved from the wrath of God, by the grace of God, for the glory of God.

THE GOSPEL TELLS US ABOUT OURSELVES:

1. IT DECLARES OUR NATURAL DEPRAVITY

The gospel reminds us daily that we were once enemies of God, without hope, destined for wrath, with no power in ourselves to change our condition or our eternal destination. Now, we are beloved children because of His great love and the redeeming power found in our Lord Jesus Christ.

2. IT DEFINES OUR NEW IDENTITY

The gospel continually reminds us the greatest and most important thing about us is we are in Christ. This is our identity. This means Christ-esteem has forever replaced self-esteem as the primary variable in our well being.

3. IT DESCRIBES OUR NEW POSITION AS SERVANTS

The gospel calls us daily to deny ourselves, identify with Christ in bearing the cross, and follow Him as joyful servants. In the gospel, we are reminded Jesus is both our Savior from sin, and the Master of our lives.

4. IT REMINDS US OF OUR NEW CITIZENSHIP

The gospel is a constant reminder this world is not our home, its success is not our goal, and its demise will not be our end. It grabs our chins and forces us to focus on eternity's promised rewards.

5. IT DEMANDS OUR PROGRESS

The gospel reminds us there is no separation between our justification and our sanctification. Whom God saves, He sanctifies. We are called to grow in the grace, knowledge, and love of Christ.

THE GOSPEL TELLS US ABOUT THE MISSION OF THE CHURCH:

1. IT DETERMINES OUR MESSAGE

The gospel keeps us planted in the biblical story and not in the changing whims of culture. It is the gospel that holds the Scriptures together, allowing them to make sense, and allowing the Church to have a meaningful message to the world, regardless of shifts in cultural norms.

2. IT CLARIFIES OUR PERSPECTIVE ON THE WORLD AROUND US

The gospel clarifies the chaos around us, reminding us the world's greatest need is not physical or emotional, but spiritual. Sinners are blind to the truth and alive to their depraved wills, and salvation only happens when the Spirit rides in on the gospel, granting regeneration, repentance, and saving faith.

3. IT SETS FORTH OUR PRIVILEGE

The gospel reminds us that, since the Spirit uses the gospel to change lives, we have the privilege of partnering with the Spirit by putting the gospel in play in the lives of those around us.

4. IT DEFINES OUR MEASURE OF SUCCESS

The gospel reminds us the job of transforming souls is completely accomplished by God and not by us. Our call is simply to be faithful in sowing the seed purely, consistently, and lovingly.

5. IT ASSURES OUR CONFIDENCE

The gospel reminds us God is the One we serve, that God is the One that saves, that His plan is right on time, and that when we are on the side of the gospel, those who reject us are actually rejecting God.

6. IT CLARIFIES OUR DOCTRINE

The gospel reminds us not all have been chosen unto salvation. Many will neither understand the truth, nor see the light. This allows us to understand why some will never accept the free offer of salvation.

7. IT DEFINES OUR ATTITUDE IN MINISTRY

The gospel reminds us God is patient and longsuffering to unruly children, helping us remember to lead and minister with grace and love, as well as truth.

8. IT DETERMINES OUR PHILOSOPHY IN MINISTRY

The gospel reminds us the mission is to grow the Kingdom, not merely increase attendance. Gospel success is first and foremost faithfulness to Christ and His Word.

9. IT RESTRICTS THE PROGRAMS OF OUR MINISTRY

The gospel keeps us from designing and delivering programs or sermons or devotional talks aimed at the will of man rather than the conscience. Ministries without a gospel core tend to produce emotional decisions rather than true saving faith, and allow unbelievers to feel better about their lives without Christ.

10. IT REJUVENATES OUR HEARTS FOR ONGOING MINISTRY

The gospel is a spring of fresh, life-giving water every day. We ignore it at our own peril. Whatever fatigue, disillusionment, or disappointment you may face, if the Spirit of God dwells in you, the gospel can be to you Heaven's great refreshment for your soul. *Drink often, and drink deeply.*

47878550R00104

Made in the USA
San Bernardino, CA
10 April 2017